KING OF RUGGER

KING OF ROGUE

Lewis Jones

KING OF RUGGER

Scratching Shed Publishing Ltd

Rugby League Classics

This edition published by Scratching Shed Publishing Ltd, 2008
Registered in England & Wales No. 6588772.
Registered office:
47 Street Lane, Leeds, West Yorkshire. LS8 1AP

www.scratchingshedpublishing.co.uk

Introduction © Phil Caplan 2008
Afterword © Scratching Shed Publishing Ltd 2008
King of Rugger © Lewis Jones

All photographs are from the personal collection of Lewis Jones.

Cover image: Lewis Jones, after receiving a pass from Brown, scores for
Leeds in a Yorkshire Cup-tie against Wakefield Trinity at Headingley. On
the left of the picture is Turnbull, the Leeds right winger. August 1955

King of Rugger was originally published by Stanley Paul & Co. in 1958

A catalogue record for this book is available from the British Library.

ISBN 978-0956007513

Typeset in Warnock Pro Semi Bold and Palatino

Printed and bound in the United Kingdom by
L.P.P.S.Ltd, Wellingborough, Northants, NN8 3PJ

Rugby League Classics

King of Rugger is the second in a new series of historically significant Rugby League Classics, rescued, re-branded and re-issued in paperback, often after having been long out-of-print.

Each Rugby League Classic comes complete with at least one original manuscript intact and contains a wealth of new and updated material, including an introductory overview by a relevant writer, evocative photographs, appendices and the modern-day recollections of those closest to the book's primary subject, i.e. family members, former team-mates and other contemporary figures.

In order to stay as true to the spirit of the original text as possible, all editing has purposely been kept to a minimum. Readers should be aware, therefore, that although factual inaccuracies by the original writer - should they occur - may be referred to and corrected in the accompanying introduction, in the main text they will be allowed to stand. In the interests of readability, however, paragraph breaks have been added where necessary, and any errors in spelling and grammar (which may well have frustrated the author at the time) now amended.

―――――――

Scratching Shed Publishing Ltd

Scratching Shed Publishing Limited is an independent publishing company founded in May 2008. We aim to produce high-quality books covering a wide range of subjects - including sport, travel and popular culture - that are of worldwide interest, yet which offer a distinctive flavour of the North of England.

Acknowledgements

The publishers are grateful for the kind permission of Lewis Jones, who allowed us to re-publish *King of Rugger* despite his humble and on-going protestations that 'no one will be interested'.

Thanks are due, too, to our own Ros Caplan, for her already customary attention to detail when transcribing the original manuscript.

Contents

Contents

INTRODUCTION

by Phil Caplan
Leeds Rhinos Heritage Officer
and leading author on the club

The titles of some sporting biographies and self-penned works make grandiose claims about the subject, but there is little doubt that, at the end of the 1956-7 rugby league season, Lewis Jones - Leeds' balding, mercurial pivot - truly was the 'King of Rugger'. His world record points haul – variously recorded as 496 in official first class matches, rising to 505 if the 21-21 draw with Hunslet in the traditional pre-season Lazenby Cup clash was included, and excluding another 73 that could have been added in three games he played for a British XIII against their French equivalents in South Africa – made him arguably one of the most famous names in the oval ball code at that moment. It was an astonishing feat, which still stands over fifty years later along with a host of club landmarks. Combined with Leeds' victory at Wembley that year, which further raised his already gilt stock although, ironically, not his points total, publishers Stanley Paul decided to have his story ghosted by a Welsh rugby journalist.

'Rugger' rather than rugby was an understandable attempt to appeal to the widest possible and then virtually untapped market for players' memoirs. His exploits as a teenager on the fervent international stage and then for the British Lions were still fresh in the memory for fifteen-a-side followers, despite his decision to 'go North' before reaching the peak of his prowess. His capture by the Loiners – a club renowned for travelling the extra mile to snare the very best – was as surprising and astonishing as it was shocking. Austerity was still the vogue in 1952 when Lewis hurriedly swapped South Wales for North Leeds, his unprecedented signing on fee of a reported £6,000 enough to buy three houses. For that, and the fact that he was only twenty-one, he carried the epithet 'Golden Boy' but the reference to the precious metal equally applied to his talent.

Wherever it glittered, it seems it also brought division provoking reverence or near disdain for a man who, after an early badly broken arm which threatened to permanently derail his new career, was never anything other than top box office. Variously described as the 'Welsh wizard' and 'maestro' or labelled infuriating, the dichotomy seemed to centre on whether he was judged by his spellbinding contributions on attack or his perceived ambivalence towards defence.

With ball in hand, there have been few finer and during his time with Leeds, a generation of fans there instantly name him as the best they ever saw; his hitch kick, floated pass and disguised scissors having gone into Headingley folk lore. He was and still is adored by a legion of blue and amber fans who marvelled at his ability to create space for others - never better illustrated than when setting up the crucial try at Wembley in 1957 for young winger Del Hodgkinson, which Lewis later claimed was the best finish he had ever seen - or to exploit the merest hint of a chance with his acceleration and glide. On top of that he was a simply wonderful goal kicker, ranking alongside the other giants of the art, Neil Fox and his fellow Welshman and later his national coach Jim Sullivan. Although the goals for club and country put him in the record books, it was undoubtedly the tries that gave him the most pleasure. That is at the heart of understanding and evaluating his genius.

Brought up in Gorseinon, from the earliest time Lewis had that odd-shaped ball in his hands - he was also good enough to be offered trials for Swansea City at soccer - he was taught that to attack and entertain was the basis for enjoyment and the key to victory. More than that, adopting the unorthodox and unpredictable, the hallmark of the greats and at which he became peerless, was to be encouraged and nurtured. Fans paid to watch the extraordinary and be entranced, they remembered the tries.

For some, though, in the typical tradition of the rugby league fan, the appreciation of seemingly effortless beauty had to be matched with the artisan, hardly surprising for a sport hewn from the honest toil of heavy industry. If fans had paid their hard-earned cash, they wanted to see their favourites working for it, especially 'celebrity' ones imported for a near incomprehensible fee and for Lewis, there was the rub. His detractors, but not his team-mates, said he either couldn't or wouldn't tackle; he was temperamental and that you could tell when he went on the field, merely by his disposition, what kind of game he would have. Much of that so-called analysis came from the fans of opposing sides who, as with any extreme talent, would have loved to have had him in their ranks. The truth was that he could and did put himself about, as he famously showed when out playing fearsome St Helens centre Doug 'come to mammy' Greenall in the 1954 Great Britain tour trial. In Australia, with either code of Lions and later when player/coach at Wentworthville, where the ability to defend is a pre-requisite for even taking the field, he was feted. He had players around him at Leeds like Keith McLellan, Harry Street and Colin Evans who could wrap up the opposition while he found the way of unlocking them.

Such a difference of opinion on the worth of a player is nothing new. Current Leeds president and learned factotum Harry Jepson OBE tells a similar tale surrounding impish half-back Alan Hardisty, in some ways a near equivalent of Lewis' at Castleford who also subsequently came to Leeds. "I was coming out of Wheldon Road one night and heard one of the locals bemoan the fact, 'that Hardisty's done nowt to'neet'. I didn't know the fellow but couldn't help myself and went up and enquired again what he had said. He confirmed that the archetypal poacher's stand-off, who appeared, to the unknowing, to be detached at times, had contributed little." That was until the wily Mr Jepson pointed out that Hardisty had scored two tries and won the game, only to get the reply, 'aye, but he's done no tacklin'. By such measure some also judged Lewis but he never understood or bothered about such earnest debate.

As esteemed *Yorkshire Post* correspondent Alfred Drewry, who delighted in so many of his performances for the blue and amber, wrote when Lewis was accorded a testimonial in 1963: "My own assessment of Jones starts with the simple statement that he is the most talented Rugby player I have ever seen. In his mastery of the ball (in flight, in his hands or at his feet); in his sense of anticipation; in his ability to read a game and bring out the best of the players alongside him he is in a class by himself. But besides giving me more pleasure than any other player I have ever watched he has also caused me more exasperation than any other. Too often in his early days one got the impression that this moody genius was not using his talents to the full. But then, if he had been one of your all-out 80-minute players in every game.....he would have burnt out years ago". [1]

Having overcome his false start with Leeds, after a clash with John Etty at Batley in January 1953 barely three months into his League career, he quickly captured the hearts of the Loiners faithful. That afternoon he had already posted a typically eye-catching touchdown, the third of his new career. Leeds aficionados loved an entertainer, having been brought up on a tradition - that still exists - of dashing enterprise, thrilling ball movement and flashing sorties down the flanks. It seemed a perfect match; a magician who could load and fire the ammunition that the adoring throng could not take your eyes off for fear of missing some audacious, unexpected skilled manoeuvre, as likely to be a disguised kick or an almost imperceptible race into space as it was the most telling and judicious of passes.

Although Warrington – who were also incredibly keen to sign him - denied Lewis a Wembley visit in 1954, his two goals Leeds' only points in a desperately disappointing semi final performance which saw them lose 8-4, there was still the same lingering question mark about his all-round contribution when it came to selection for the touring party that year. He had already been a sensation four years earlier with the Union Lions and although he did become a dual code international against Australia at the Sydney Cricket Ground in the opening Test, and played fifteen more times for Great Britain, his versatility at that level proved to be a curse. Having been selected as a centre, the position he favoured, he played the majority of the tour at full-back and debuted against the Kangaroos on the wing, going on to score a record number of points in a fixture between the old foes and overall on tour. His final caps came during the disappointing 1957 World Cup campaign, again in Australia, at stand-off and, certainly, he did not have the kind of representative career that his wonderful talents merited, although he was always the major draw card. There was a huge irony that on the back of his record breaking domestic season and cup winner's medal that was the season his international appearances came to an ignominious end but that was Lewis, ever the capricious.

He was a master footballer guaranteeing virtually eight points every time he set foot on a field even though, initially, he was second choice kicker to New Zealander Bert Cook when he arrived at Headingley. Astonishing though his records are – he still holds the goals and points high in a career for Leeds - statistics do not tell his tale and mean little to him, even now. He is disarmingly reticent and humbly modest about his achievements or why people should be interested in them after so long.

According to the doyen of written and broadcast commentators, Eddie Waring, in his 1968 tome *The Great Ones*: "No player in the long and colourful history of the Leeds club had such an individual following. Almost to a man the Leeds fans 'worshipped' him. He was, without doubt, a superb craftsman and master tactician, though apt to make spectators incredulous that such a gifted exponent of the rugby arts could lapse into 'casualness'". [2]

There is an iconic picture of a slight, sandy-haired Lewis arriving at Headingley from Upper Lime Street in his home town for his first training session and being taught how to play the ball by Arthur Clues, with Jeff Stevenson acting as dummy half. That was some triumvirate but, as so often in the colourful history of the club, truly great individuals did not make a regularly winning team. Wembley success in 1957 did not build a dynasty and it was only in 1961, three

years after Lewis had written *King of Rugger* and coming
towards the end of his initial ten-year deal, that the parts
gradually became an increasingly formidable whole. After
three seasons of finishing fourteenth, something clicked and
for the first time in the club's history, they finished top at the
end of the regular season, winning thirty of their thirty-six
weekly fixtures. Playing almost two-thirds of his club games
at centre, by then he was ensconced at stand-off from where
he captained the side exhibiting his guile, mastery and
perceptiveness to greatest effect.

Critics claimed that an easier fixture list, where they had
avoided facing the two big Lancashire outfits of St Helens
and Warrington, had elevated the Loiners into a false
position, but Lewis was at his impish best giving Alex
Murphy the runaround as Saints were seen off at
Headingley, thanks to two wonder tries from the 'flying
dentist' Wilf Rosenberg, in the play-off semi-final. Five times
Leeds had made the Championship decider, Huddersfield
in three of them, Swinton and Hunslet in their previous
appearance some twenty-three years earlier denying them
the most valued prize. At Odsal, against a star-studded
Warrington outfit, Lewis led his men to the long-promised
land with a virtuoso skipper's display. Early on, he dropped
the ball with the line open, but his pinpoint kicking and
varied distribution quickly eroded the Wire's resistance to
more than repay that unprecedented initial outlay.

It was a precious moment, Leeds fans haring across the
famous bowl at the final whistle to hug and chair their
heroes, while some of the older generation who, perhaps,
had thought they would never witness such a scene, stared
misty-eyed from the cavernous terraces. Over thirty years
later, the enormity of the achievement was not lost on the
skipper. "To be the first Leeds captain to lift the
Championship Trophy was the highlight of my career and

gave me more pleasure than anything. In the 1950s and 1960s I think most players, and perhaps even the clubs themselves, considered a good run in the Challenge Cup more attractive and more lucrative, but for me the Championship has always been the more important. A few good matches and plenty of luck can take a side to Wembley, but you need more than that to win a League Championship. The Championship is the true test of a side." [3]

His superbly swept passes that almost negated the Warrington pack and dazzling footwork would have won him the man of the match award if it had existed then, as he and fellow Welshman Colin Evans outplayed opposite numbers Jackie Edwards, father of modern day great Shaun, and Bobby Greenough. It was a virtuoso display. "We were not the greatest of teams, but we did have a winning spirit and a perfect blend of players. Only my first-ever union international for Wales against England at Twickenham would come anywhere near to this Championship decider. The sort of moment that makes rugby worth playing." [4]

The only sadness was that his football chairman, Rex Proctor, was not there to see the historic moment that he had helped create, having been tragically killed in a car accident a few weeks before in Lewis' native South Wales. Victory was dedicated to his memory.

A contract extension and a testimonial that raised a massive £2,000 followed, Lewis leaving for the sun of Sydney in Easter 1964 to a rapturous send off, his stint in the southern hemisphere seeing him garner another 1,000 points. He left Leeds with an astonishing overall record that may never be surpassed; 385 appearances, 144 tries, 1,244 goals and 2,920 points. On 231 occasions he took the field as a centre, 117 at stand-off, 35 filling in at full-back and once on each wing, such was his versatility.

Today, he is still a great supporter of the Leeds club, does not miss many games, is a Taverner and spends a lot of his time up at Horsforth Golf Club in the company of friends who remember only too well what a wonderful asset he was and continues to be for the game. If Celtic Crusaders, on their elevation to Super League in 2009, could find one from near home like him, how fortunate they would be.

Perhaps the best placed people to sum up the contribution of one of the code's finest ever exponents, rather than those who were merely privileged to witness his incredible deeds or hear tales spun of his majesty, are his often wondrous team-mates. Closest at hand during the bulk of his days at Leeds was Keith McLellan. For Lewis's testimonial brochure, the Australian hard man concocted the following ode in tribute to his centre partner.

Lewis "Dai Bach" Jones

by KEITH McLELLAN, 11-6-62

Of all the players I have seen,
And many great ones there have been,
The one who clearly leads the rest,
Who measures up to any test;
The one that I would rate the best
IS LEWIS 'DAI BACH' JONES.

Let's take the kick: an important skill,
Punts, drop-kicks, goals, he kicked at will
Whether on attack or in defence,
His boot was always found immense,
To relieve a situation tense,
Came LEWIS 'DAI BACH' JONES.

And then there is that pair of hands
Like a magnet on which the ball just lands;
High in the air or low to the ground
He'd swoop on the ball without a sound,
The whole team then he'd run around,
LEWIS 'DAI BACH' JONES.

This brings me to that change of pace
With which to the line he'd often race,
Almost a goose-step some did say;
Whatever it was, it paved the way
To often earn us winning pay,
LEWIS 'DAI BACH' JONES.

Some say his defence was not up to scratch,
His other skills it didn't match,
But if he wished the game to save
He'd tackle all about him brave,
Then listen to the critics rave,
Of LEWIS 'DAI BACH' JONES.

And after all is said and done,
And Lewis has had his final run,
Who stood out above them all?
A footballer who was ten feet tall;
They've even heard of him in Whitehall,
LEWIS 'DAI BACH' JONES.

--

Lewis never understood such fuss. He loved playing the game in the way he thought it was meant to be expressed; with panache, flamboyance and the risk to entertain. Still fiercely proud of his roots, he loves Leeds and the club that played such a huge part in his life. So much so that his e-mail address includes the word Loiner.

[1] Quoted in *Gone North Volume 2* by Robert Gate, R. Gate,1988

[2] *Rugby League, The Great Ones* by Eddie Waring, Pelham, 1969

[3] Quoted in *The Match Of My Life* complied by Ray French, Headline, 1994

[4] Ibid

Original frontispiece (1958)

Lewis Jones is to the Rugby world what Stanley Matthews is to Soccer, Keith Miller to Cricket and Sugar Ray Robinson to Boxing. In this racy and absorbing book the outstanding post-war star of Rugby Union and Rugby League football tells his life story.

His dramatic rise to fame from schoolboy football in the Gower Peninsula of South Wales to leading points scorer in Wales' first Triple Crown winning side for 39 years is a fascinating story. Even more interesting is the dramatic hunt for his services by Rugby League clubs, and his eventual 'signing' at a record fee.

After turning professional he has become the greatest box office star in Rugby League football. In this book he compares both codes and tells the innermost secrets of the two games. In 1956-57 he gained the greatest triumph of his career when he became the first League player to score 500 points in a season.

All his life Lewis Jones has had a flair for rising to the big occasion, and the writing of his autobiography is no exception to that rule. He remains a top box office personality in every way. From West Wales to New South Wales his name is a household word.

King of Rugger

1

HOW IT ALL BEGAN

In rugby football, no less perhaps than in other games, the gap between failure and success is a narrow one. That I suppose will strike you as a pretty commonplace remark, yet I am nevertheless able to recall a score of important matches that have been decided by seemingly trifling incidents - a dropped pass, a lucky bounce, or a veneer of paint on a goalpost.

In fact it all makes me wonder just how much of the success I have been fortunate enough to achieve, both as an amateur and as a professional, I can attribute to a split-second decision taken at (what was for me, at any rate) a fairly tense and vital moment of the final Welsh Trial match played at Cardiff Arms Park on January 7th, 1950. The circumstances, I've no doubt, will be readily recalled by Welshmen - Wales were on the lookout for a full-back replacement for Cardiff's Frank Trott who had recently retired - the choice it seems, finally resting between myself and the cool, efficient London Welsh no.1, Gerwyn Williams. Frankly I didn't fancy my chances a great deal that afternoon at Cardiff for, all other things being equal, I reasoned the Selectors were likely to plump for the experienced player, and that certainly wasn't me, for I had only six months of first-class rugger behind me, and most of that as centre three-quarter. For the moment, however, it was enough for me that I was out there on the Arms Park duelling with Gerwyn for a place against England, and the prize that every Welsh schoolboy covets, the red velvet cap with the silver braid and tassels and the magic inscription W.R.U. If I was pessimistic to begin with, my confidence mounted as the game went on, for my kicks were going where I intended them, I was making no serious errors in either catching or fielding, and, most comforting of all, there in front of me were the game's two most formidable tacklers, Bleddyn Williams and Jack Matthews.

Everything in fact seemed to be going far better than I dared even hope, when suddenly out of the murk that envelops the Arms Park on a January afternoon came the squat and speeding figure of the Maesteg wing three-quarter, Windsor Major, who had been capped for Wales the previous winter.

Even before I'd grasped the situation he was bearing down on me inside our twenty-five; fleetingly I remembered my old school coach Bill Bowen's remarks about 'shepherding wing three-quarters to the touchline', but even as I did so I realised that I had already given Windsor all the room he needed. There was only one thing for it - I just threw myself blindly in his speeding direction. For one heart-clutching moment I had the illusion of grasping thin air, then the impact, jarring as it was, reassured me I'd made it, and there were the both of us sprawled untidily on (for me) the side of the corner flag that mattered.

You will understand perhaps why I still speculate on the effect of that tackle. If I had missed it, would I, I wonder, have been picked for Wales at Twickenham? Or even if I had my chance at some later date, would the gods have served me as well as they did on the afternoon of my actual debut in international rugger? Deep down inside me I still believe that my whole career was shaped by that rather fortuitous tackle of Windsor Major on the Arms Park eight years ago; that, too, might explain how it comes that I am sometimes accused of a 'couldn't care less attitude' towards the game.

Believe me, that is not true - it's just that I'm alive to the fact that the 'rub of the green' can work both ways. Why then, I tell myself, go into ecstasies or be unduly depressed by one or a series of incidents that depend so much upon pure luck and coincidence?

* * * * *

Rugby football, or for that matter sport as a whole, started for me long before I kicked a ball of any description. Ours was a real sporting household, for not only was my family - my brothers Cliff and Alun, and my sister Enid - brought up within throwing distance of the Gorseinon cricket and football ground, but the conversation at meal-times, indeed at most times, seemed to centre on one game or another.

There was, to be sure, no lack of topics in a village as sports-minded as Gorseinon, for Ivor Jones (nowadays a Welsh Rugby Union selector), Iorwerth Jones, an international at rugby and almost one at soccer, Bryn Howells, a magnificent full-back and first-class cricketer, Jim Lang, the outstanding international line-out specialist of his period, not to speak of the fabulous Charles Hallows, who once startled the first-class cricket world by scoring a thousand runs in May, all either lived in, or had strong connections with, the village. Needless to say, their achievements as recounted by my father and my brothers were calculated to send a schoolboy's fancy racing rather too far from the classroom than his elders were sometimes prepared to tolerate. Indeed I don't think any schoolboy ever had more encouragement to take an interest in sport than I did.

My father especially was keen on both rugby and cricket, and then, to fire my interest still further, there was the example of my brothers - Cliff, who (until a wartime injury sustained on service with the R.A.F. put paid to his football) played at full-back for both Llanelly and Swansea besides playing cricket for the Gorseinon Works team in the summer, and Alun, who later, to my intense delight, played with me for both Neath and Llanelly.

Alun, too, was a good cricketer, but even today there are local folk who tell me that my eldest brother Cliff was the best all-round sportsman amongst the Jones family of Lime Street, Gorseinon, but as I was only eight years old when he hung up his boots for the last time in 1939, I can hardly hazard an opinion on that. What I can remember, however, even though dimly as a youngster in short pants, is the furore which resulted at Lime Street when a Rugby League agent and a couple of club directors called around to offer him £300, a sizeable sum pre-war, to sign on as a professional. Little did I think that less than fifteen years later, with a major world war behind us, my family would once again be repulsing Rugby League agents - this time on my behalf, and with a world-record fee as the bait.

My folks tell me that I was never without either a bat or ball in my hand as a youngster, and that I used to haunt the Gorseinon ground whenever there was a cricket or rugger match in progress. They are probably right at that, but my first introduction to organised team games was effected at the Gowerton County School where coach Bill Bowen had me at full-back in the school 'B' team almost before I'd got my bearings in this famous 'rugger' academy, which had produced three famous internationals in the persons of Rowe Harding, Haydn Tanner, and his cousin and half-back partner, W.H.T. Davies.

Captain of the 'B' team during the period was Gwynne Walters who was, according to a photograph in my possession, even smaller than I. Gwynne has, or course, subsequently become one of the leading Rugby Union referees in the country. Indeed his control of the last university match at Twickenham can only be the prelude to international honours. Certainly Gwynne knew his rugby backwards even as a schoolboy, and were it not for injury might have gained as outstanding a reputation as a player as he most certainly has as a referee.

Like so many other youngsters who came under his wing, I owe a lot to Bill 'Bow' - as we used to call him - for his wise counsel in what were our formative years, but he will, I'm sure, pardon me for the (to many, no doubt) seemingly heretical belief that no amount of coaching can ever make a player out of someone who lacks natural talent and aptitude.

I perhaps was lucky in that the game of rugby, in many of its aspects at least, came more or less easily to me. If follows that I shall always be eternally grateful to Mr. Bowen for resisting what must have been a temptation to mould my play along more orthodox lines. That, I think, is the hallmark of a great coach - to be able to correct the more obvious faults in a player's technique without interfering with his natural style and outlook.

I have just stated that most aspects of the game came easily to me, and so they did, but believe me, neither in my own case nor, to my knowledge, in anyone else's does that mean that a player can dispense with practice. Take goal-kicking, for instance - I've kicked a few in my time, but I wouldn't have landed the half of them, had I not practised and practised to the point of sheer boredom and monotony.

It is true that my kicking technique is adapted to suit myself, but whether or not it conforms to the textbooks on the subject doesn't really matter, for as far as I was able I've perfected it with practice. That I was able to do so I owe, in great measure, to the tolerance, patience, and terrific enthusiasm of my lifelong friend Louis Gazzi, who, in the days when we were in the Gowerton School and Welsh Secondary School's XV together, used to accompany me on hour-long practice sessions on the Gorseinon ground.

With Louis as 'placer' we'd start off on the twenty-five, and work back to the half-way line, kicking from almost every angle. If I missed a kick from any particular angle with more frequency than I felt was justified, we'd retrieve the ball, talk over things in an effort to discover where we were going wrong, and then essay the kick until I could plonk it over with something approaching regularity. I owe a great debt to Louis Gazzi in this respect, for such lessons, I'm sure would have been both physically and mentally intolerable had I been on my own.

They were happy and sport-crammed days that I spent at the Gowerton County School. In the winter mornings, I'd play at full-back for the School XV, and in the afternoon as a centre-forward for the Gorseinon, Thistles A.F.C. in local Junior League games. Indeed at the time I was very much torn between the two games, and even today I seize the opportunity to watch a good-class game of soccer.

Strange to relate, I might quite easily have been a professional with Swansea Town even before I entered second-class rugby with Gorseinon. After one game in which I was fortunate enough to bang ten 'laid-on' goals into the opponent's netting, I was approached by the late Mr. Glyn Evans, the club's scout, with a view to signing for Swansea Town as an amateur. My father would have none of this, and what is more there and then invited me to choose between the two games. He said he didn't really mind which, but it would have to be one or the other.

As things turned out I plumped for rugger, and in season 1947-8 gained a place in the Welsh Secondary School XV which played against France at the Cardiff Arms Park. I was a full-back, my customary position in those days, and captaining us that afternoon was the Gwendraeth Valley outside-half, Caerwyn James, who, even in those days, was a classical-looking player and a really brilliant attacker. Strangely enough, especially since he has sustained his schoolboy form in first-class rugby with both Llanelly and the London Welsh, Caerwyn has, to date, only played once in the Welsh senior side - against Australia at Cardiff in 1958 - ten years after his schoolboy debut. Also in the side that afternoon were several players whom knowledgeable judges picked out as internationals of the future, but as things turned out only myself and Trevor Brewer of Newport High School actually made the grade.

There again you have the luck of the game, for I've no doubt that Ken Jones and Roy Bish of Aberavon would both have been capped as seniors had fortune favoured them to the same extent as it did me. So much indeed can depend on pure coincidence, as for example when one turns in a 'blinder' on the day the Selectors are out in force, or plays one's worst games away from the selectorial eye. Equally, of course, the luck can go the other way.

Rugby football, though, was not my sole interest in those days, for the summer months were apt to be as crowded as those in the winter. As with rugger, it was very much the same story - cricket for Gowerton School in the morning, for the Gorseinon Works second eleven in the afternoons, and, for good measure, a lot of athletics as well.

I made several good cricket scores, including a couple of centuries for both the school and the works teams, and I was naturally elated to notch a schoolboy 'double' by gaining a place in the Welsh Secondary Schools XI, and more so at being awarded the captaincy. Incidentally in the Gowerton School XI of my period was a slight fair-haired youngster by name of Onllwyn Brace - a name that nowadays rings a bell or two in Rugby Union circles.

Indeed, looking back I'm sure that it was cricket that was my first love at that time; if anything, I then obtained rather more fun out of hitting sixes and hurling the ball down as fast as I was able, than I did out of punting a rugger ball to touch or banging it over a cross-bar. Not, however, that I was confronted with any choice - on the contrary my sporting future was decided for me.

2

INTO THE BIG TIME

Leaving the Gowerton County School at the end of the summer term of 1948, I was fortunate enough, through the good offices of my friend John Deeley and others, to obtain a clerical job with the Divisional Health Board at Swansea.

With my Saturday afternoons free I immediately commenced playing for my village club, Gorseinon, in the West Wales League Championship competition. Alongside me in the centre was, as usual, my chum and goal-kicking collaborator Louis Gazzi. Nor was that the only thing I owe to Louis in the football sense, for he was a wonderful chap to play alongside; indeed but for injuries and the considerable responsibility of running the family cafeteria business, he would have added a senior cap to the one he gained as a secondary schoolboy.

Captaining the side was Hermas Evans, who has since earned fame as the man who did most to establish the Welsh Youth Rugby Union, whilst others who helped me considerably in bridging the gap from schoolboy to adult rugger were Will Lane, a former Llanelly stalwart and in those days our club secretary, and Adrian Walters, who had been playing rugger and cricket for Gorseinon before the majority of us were born. With youth and experience nicely blended, it was indeed a pretty useful side we had at Gorseinon in that rather bitter winter of 1948-9, and I consequently had far more opportunities to shine than I might have had in a side that went in wholesale for the kick-and-rush tactics that are supposed to be the main feature of second-class rugby in Wales.

Indeed this strikes me about as good a time as any to deny the accusation that cup and championship football is *always* a crude and violent affair.

Although, in the West Wales Union at least, the accent is largely on forward play, it is not exclusively so, and many teams produce a very high standard of open and attractive football. Fortunately, as I say, for me personally, Gorseinon in those days happened to be one of them. I cannot let the occasion pass either without paying tribute to the inestimable value of the West Wales Rugby Union as a breeding ground for senior football. Its hurly burly and quite often fiercely competitive element sharpen a young player's reactions, and generally assist him in bridging the very wide gap that exists between schoolboy and first-class rugby.

By Christmas, 1948, I had - mainly through goal-kicking - eighty-eight points in the scoring bag for Gorseinon, and there were, inevitably I suppose, rumours that some of the first-class clubs in the neighbourhood were beginning to take an interest in my progress. In fact the first offer came from Swansea, but unfortunately the weather intervened to cause the cancellation of the match in which I was to have worn the famous white jersey.

I make no secret now of the fact that I would dearly have loved to play for this very old and distinguished rugby club, for although I have been royally treated by the other Welsh clubs I later played for, I did in fact cherish a schoolboy ambition to play for the club that had produced such legendary names as Trew, Bancroft, Owen, Claude Davey, Hayden Tanner, and Willy Davies. While, however, I was hopefully awaiting a second invitation from St Helens, the Neath club stepped in and asked me to turn out for them in a midweek game with London Hospital. Needless to say I jumped at the chance, and as things turned out, fortune was doubly kind to me on that cold January afternoon at the Gnoll ground, for not only was I able to contribute twelve of the twenty-four points that were the margin of Neath's victory, but the Welsh selectors, out in force having a look at Neath's flying wingman Keith Maddocks, were there to see me do it.

I am not of course assuming that I made any lasting impression on the selectors with a debut which, after all, was made in the most favourable circumstances, but I do feel that it perhaps helped them to recall me more readily to mind when I was playing my rugger with the Devonport Services outside the borders of Wales.

The following Saturday Neath were due at Herne Hill in London to play the London Welsh, and although we were convincingly defeated I again had a double satisfaction. Apart from scoring Neath's only try, I had the additional thrill of playing in the same side as my brother Alun, who had moved from Llanelly to join me at the Gnoll.

After the London Welsh match came an away match at Penarth, and with it the very first of the several records I have been fortunate enough to establish in rugby football.

I shall always look back on the tiny Penarth Athletic ground with a special affection, for luck always seemed to go my way when I played there with the Barbarians at Easter. Certainly I had a fair share of it on the afternoon of my first visit, for by scoring eighteen points (three tries, a penalty, and three conversions) I was able to equal the Neath club record established several years earlier by the Welsh international wing three-quarter Howell Jones, who had once scored six tries against Neath's great rivals, Aberavon.

I had now accumulated a total of thirty-three points in my first three matches of first-class football; even so I did not share the generally expressed opinion that I had finally 'arrived' in the top bracket. My success, such as it was, had, as I well knew, been achieved against opposition that by no stretch of the imagination could be described as 'formidable'. Then too I had a feeling that I had enjoyed more than my portion of the luck that proverbially goes to beginners.

What in fact I was looking forward to, though with pretty mixed feelings, was my first major inter-club clash, for this, I considered, would supply the 'acid' test of my ability to make a go of first-class rugby. I did not have long to wait, for the second match I played for Neath at the Gnoll was against none other than those famous 'Red Devil' from the West - Llanelly.

Here then was my first taste of club rivalry at its fiercest, and as I stripped in the dressing-room beneath the stand I could almost sense the tenseness and expectancy of the waiting crowd as hundreds of feet drummed a tattoo on the floor of the stand. It was a slightly unnerving experience, and although I have subsequently travelled the rugby football world from Twickenham to Wooloongabba, I don't think I have ever encountered any crowd which can so tangibly communicate their own fervour and partisanship to the players themselves.

Fortunately, however, one has in most cases little time to

dwell on 'atmospheres', and this was one of them, for straight from the kick-off the scarlet jerseys (scarlet, I fancy, always heightens the impression of fervour and ferocity) were swarming menacingly around our goal-line. If one has butterflies in the stomach before a big match, they are, I find, quickly dispelled at the first touch of the ball or physical contact with an opponent. So it proved during the course of this - my first major Welsh club encounter.

A pick-up at the feet of the forwards, and a relieving kick which won the applause of the crowd - the Neath faction of it at any rate - restored my poise, and in no time at all I was unconscious of either crowd or atmosphere. In fact within minutes of the kick-off I had fielded a misdirected touch-finder from one of the Llanelly defenders and crossed over in the corner.

The simplicity of it surprised me, and here I think is a lesson that can be of tremendous value to any young player who is faced with the ordeal of a debut in first-class football, or for that matter in any kind of sport. Briefly it is this - respect your opponent by all means, but do not be overawed by reputations. Remember that the seasoned international is only human and like yourself prone to error, so when you see a Big Name perpetrate some unmentionable crudity, or fail to execute a simple duty, do not stand and stare in blank incredulity! On the contrary, dash in and capitalise on your good fortune.

In the Llanelly match, my unexpected try put me on great terms with myself and most certainly gave me the confidence I needed, for near the end I was able to break away down the touchline to put in a cross kick from which Roy John, not an international in those days, scored a try near the posts which I was able to convert. Needless to say, I was well pleased with the results of what I considered to be the 'fiery' part of my baptism in first-class rugby.

King of Rugger

For the rest of the 1948-9 season I played at centre three-quarter for Neath, and, on a few occasions, for the Glamorgan County XV. This is as good a time as any to pay a tribute to the advice and encouragement I received from the Neath players and committeemen. Treasurer Theo Davies and committee member Bert Sutcliffe are names which come instantly to mind in this respect, and certainly no club ever possessed a player who was more friendly or accommodating towards those younger than himself than Rhys Stephens who, football ability apart, was an asset to any team for the tremendous influence he exerted in the dressing-room. I was delighted too, after my departure to Leeds, to hear that Vivian Evans had created a scoring record for Wales in his first and only season of international rugger, for Viv too was a great team man, and a fine full-back into the bargain.

Reading, as I sometimes do nowadays, through the accumulation of cuttings collected by the various members of my family, I never fail to be impressed with the kindness with which I was treated by the Press during my salad days in first-class rugby. In most cases the Press boys, I feel, are sincerely anxious to give the young player every encouragement they can, even if it sometimes entails a spot of mild exaggeration *en route*. A cynic might say, of course, that journalists are equally adept at knocking their subjects off the pedestals they have erected for them, and certainly I have had my own ups and downs in that respect. By and large, however, I consider that the Press of Great Britain give their sporting subjects a far fairer deal than in several of the countries I have visited. However, more of this subject anon.

What in fact prompted this trend of thought was the newspaper cuttings I've just mentioned. Reading through them I find that I topped the century of points for Neath during a match against Swansea at St Helens, which might suggest that I was well satisfied with the results of my first three months in the first-class game. So I was, but neither my success nor the several rather flattering predictions made on my behalf, I can assure you, caused me to think in terms of international rugby.

On the contrary, when during the summer months I received a letter from the Admiralty ordering me to report for National Service with the Royal Navy, I imagined that my rugby football for the next couple of winters would be restricted to minor club and inter-unit games. As it happened I was wrong; exactly how wrong though I could never even have imagined, even in my wildest dreams.

3

TWICKENHAM AND A TRIPLE CROWN

Stationed at the naval shore establishment H.M.S. *Fisgard* in Devonport, I had, needless to say, ample opportunity for playing the games of my particular choice, and I shall always cherish the memory of those carefree, 'sport-crammed days' of the years between 1949-51.

It was as a member of the Devonport Services XV that I first became associated with Malcolm Thomas, subsequently my colleague in so many thrilling games for Wales, the Barbarians, and with the Lions in Australia and New Zealand. They don't come any finer than Malcolm either as footballers or gentlemen, and I regard my friendship with him as having a great formative influence on my career in Rugby Union.

Only recently my great friend, and present Leeds manager, told me that one of his greatest disappointments was that he had been unable to induce Malcolm to come over to the Rugby League along with myself, and I cannot but echo his regret. Malcolm is more than a brilliant football player - he is a team man in every sense of the word, and a lovable personality in to the bargain.

During our Devonport days Malcolm was a lieutenant instructor on H.M.S. *Raleigh*, whilst I was a Stores Assistant on *Fisgard*, and at once we struck up a happy and profitable partnership in the centre for the Services XV.

I revelled in the more carefree atmosphere of English club football for, in contrast to Wales where the 'needle' element is so often a deterrent to experiment and adventure, I was encouraged to try all manner of tricks and subterfuges, many of which, I can assure you, I'd never dream of reproducing in say a Llanelly-Swansea encounter. In many instances, too, I got away with them, and although my doing so may possibly have made me a little cocksure on occasions, I do not think that this in the end redounded to my disadvantage.

Confidence, as opposed to arrogance, is not, as I think you will agree, a bad thing in a rugby player, and I am accordingly convinced that the 'licence' I was sometimes permitted on the Rectory ground at Devonport engendered in me a faith in my ability that has since served me in good stead during both my amateur and professional career. Indeed, I'm sure rugby football would benefit inestimably were its young players allowed to serve their 'apprenticeships' in an environment in which results are of secondary consideration.

The first hint that the people back at home had not entirely lost sight of me came, quite unexpectedly, in the shape of an invitation to turn out in the second Welsh Trial match which was to be played at Aberavon eight days before Christmas of 1949. I say unexpectedly because, although my form for the Services had won me a great deal of praise in the West country newspapers, I had no reason to believe that the Welsh selectors were likely to be impressed, even if they'd read the articles concerned.

With Jack Matthews, Bleddyn Williams, and Malcolm

King of Rugger

Thomas all available, the centre three-quarter position struck me as being the least of their problems. It was not, however, as a centre that the Welsh Rugby Union required my presence at the Aberavon Trial, but rather as one of the candidates for the full-back position vacated by Cardiff's Frank Trott at the end of the previous season. The other candidate was the Port Talbot-born London Welsh player Gerwyn Williams, and in retrospect, I should say we broke about even at Aberavon that afternoon; in any event, the Selectors picked us both again for the final trial at Cardiff in the early New Year, when I finally got the vote, though, as I've related, not without a palpitation or so.

So it came about that, on a beautifully mild January afternoon a fortnight later, I followed John Gwilliam and the rest of my team mates out into the babble of noise and excitement that surrounded the verdant green turf of Twickenham. The years make a blur of individual memories and impressions, but no player, I imagine, ever forgets his first international match - certainly I never will.

Even now as I write in remote Yorkshire I can savour anew the thrill of pride that tingled through my whole being as the Welsh trainer, Ray Lewis, handed me the scarlet jersey with the three feathers gleaming silvery against the sombre background of the dressing-room. I can feel again that sinking feeling in the pit of the stomach as I stood with the rest of the lads for the playing of the National Anthems. I recall too John Gwilliam - he must have been a psychologist as well as a great captain and footballer - handing me the bright yellow ball, with the instruction, 'Far downfield as you can, Lewis.' I took him at his word, kicked deep into the England twenty-five, and the battle was on.

Welshmen in particular will recall the background to the Twickenham match of 1950, which was not, to say the least, an encouraging one.

Twickenham And A Triple Crown

Wales, to begin with, had been, for one of the rare occasions in history, 'Wooden Spoonists' the previous winter, and to judge from the volume of criticism which greeted the announcement of the chosen XV few seemed to think that there was anything better in store for us this time. Finally to send the hopes of my countrymen lower than the deepest pit in the all the Rhondda were the withdrawals, on the eve of the game, of first Rhys Stephens, and then, at the very eleventh hour, of the chosen skipper, Bleddyn Williams. Worse still, we were five points in arrears within ten minutes of the start when, as our passing broke down inside our own half of the field, the England right wing intervened and fairly streaked for the corner. The speed and suddenness of the whole manoeuvre left both Trevor Brewer and myself almost stranded, and although I got to grips with Smith at the corner flag his impetus swept him over for a try which Hofmeyer converted.

It was now, however, that John Gwilliam revealed for the first time his mettle as a leader; in no time at all he had his forwards whipped to a fury and hammering hard at the English goal-line. Behind them, fair-haired Billy Cleaver, kicking with superb judgement, marshaled the backs magnificently, so that I felt we must score from any one of the furious melées that waged within the England twenty-five. However, I hardly expected to be the architect of the score I was sure would come any moment, yet that's the way it happened.

Harassed by a couple of Welshmen, Murray Hofmeyer failed to carry the touchline on the right-hand side of the field in our half, and as I retrieved the ball and shaped to make the angle for my own line kick, I noticed that the England follow up was neither as speedy nor as collective as I had expected. Taking advantage of this, I moved quickly infield, dummied left to decoy a couple of late arrivals, switched right, and raced through a gap right up to the England twenty-five, where I found the supporting forwards at my elbow. Inevitably (as I was later to discover) chunky Cliff Davies of Cardiff was one of them, and he it was who took the final pass and scored, amid a din that seemed likely to lift the roofs off the Twickenham stands - not to mention the violent oscillations it produced in the radio sets back in Welsh Wales. I missed that goal kick, but early in the second half was able to bang over a penalty and convert a try scored by that magnificent back-row forward Ray Cale. We had won 11-5, and I will never forget the thrill of being 'chaired' off the field along with skipper John Gwilliam by our exultant countrymen.

Twickenham indeed has an atmosphere of its own, for no one but the most insensitive of persons can fail to be impressed there. The towering stands convey an impression of grandeur, and in some queer, indefinable way one seems conscious of the fact that the ground really is the headquarters of the game the world over. Why this is so I cannot explain, but from my own experience at least even the vast stadiums of Eden Park, New Zealand, or the Sydney cricket ground, Australia, never seem to impress one in quite the same way. Twickenham, too, has always been kind to me as a player, for apart from the thrill of my international debut there, I invariably seemed to do well there playing for the Navy in inter-Service matches.

While on the subject of Twickenham, I might say that I am often asked whether I found that the fact that the ground is enclosed on three of its sides by huge stands had an effect on my kicking. My answer is that I have not found it abnormally so, for although the eddies, swirls, vacuums, and the rest do, on enclosed grounds, exercise a certain influence on the flight and trajectory of the kicked ball, this is not I think an overriding influence; at Twickenham, as on all grounds, one can, if one takes the trouble, quickly size up and allow for any such peculiarities.

Twickenham And A Triple Crown

The Twickenham victory had of course boosted Welsh morale enormously, with the result that players and followers alike looked forward to the Scottish match at St Helens, Swansea, with every confidence. As things turned out we were too strong for the Scots, particularly forward, but for me personally the game was something of an anti-climax. Having looked forward so eagerly to putting on a good show before my own people, especially the kind of folk of Gorseinon who had turned out *en masse* for the occasion, I then proceeded to give a performance as mediocre as any I can remember.

Nothing seemed to go right for me that afternoon, and I thank my lucky stars that Jack Matthews in front of me was at his brave, crash-tackling best - even now I can hear the impact with which he repeatedly crashed into Scotland's burly wing, Doug Smith, as he churned for the corner flag like some Sherman tank run amok.

Billy Cleaver, for his part, will remember the occasion as one of the very rare ones on which he was cheered by a Swansea crowd. He dropped a goal for Wales, which of course is a vastly different matter from dropping one on behalf of the mortal enemy, Cardiff - in the estimation of a Swansea crowd, that is. The important thing though was that we had won, and consequently paved the way to the goal coveted above all others, the Rugby Union Triple Crown.

Ireland, captained by Karl Mullen, were now the last obstacle between an objective that had eluded Welsh XVs for forty years, so you can imagine the tension and taut expectancy that penetrated the dressing-rooms at Ravenhill, Belfast, as we stripped in readiness for what was surely the most important match Wales had contested since the famous New Zealand affray at Cardiff in 1935. This time I was at centre, Gerwyn Williams getting his first cap at full-back, and Malcolm Thomas moving to the wing to allow for the reshuffle.

King of Rugger

As usual John Gwilliam implemented his own ideas of psychological warfare by throwing our dressing-room door wide open so that the Irish team could hear our singing, and of course be impressed accordingly by our complete composure. Certainly we needed every device, psychological or otherwise, we could command, for the Irish who had won the Crown themselves in two consecutive seasons were a formidable team indeed. Superbly led by Mullen, their forwards were a unit every bit as compact and mobile as were our own; in the red-haired McCarthy they had a wing-forward capable of capitalizing swiftly on the smallest error of the opposition, and, above all, they possessed in Jack Kyle one of the really great footballers and strategists of modern times.

I have of course heard it argued that the one outstanding feature of Kyle's football was his ability to kick accurately in support of his forwards, and I agree that it was this aspect of his play which was most frequently in evidence in the home internationals in which Ireland were engaged. In New Zealand and Australia, however, I saw Jackie produce a brand of attacking rugby which to my mind at least establishes him as the greatest stand-off half in modern rugby. Certainly, in peak form and fitness I'd have modest Jackie Kyle in any World XV of my choice.

So it was that two superbly fit and aggressively confident teams faced each other at Ravenhill, Belfast, on the sunny and otherwise memorable afternoon of March 11th, 1950. This was a battle if ever there was one, and right through the first thrill-packed half a case of 'Greek meets Greek', for the two packs conceded nothing to each other on points of power and ferocity, whilst behind them the backs largely cancelled each other. It was Jack Matthews who eventually broke the strangle-hold - and in typical fashion - for as the ball went loose in mid-field Jack was there to gather and thrust past a couple of opponents with a heave of his powerful shoulders. A few incisive strides, and the ball flashed out to Ken Jones, who sped for the corner in real Olympic style. A wonderful try which unfortunately I did not manage to convert.

A penalty goal from George Norton enabled Ireland to draw level soon after half-time, and with the scores equal the battle waged even more furiously, and had it not been for a quite incredible intervention by Billy Cleaver over his own goal-line McCarthy must assuredly have scored after Kyle had split our defence with one of his devilishly placed short punts. Only two minutes were left for play when a scrum went down on the Irish twenty-five for Ireland to heel on their own head. However, as the ball flashed out to Kyle, Ray Cale was on him simultaneously, the impact of his tackle jolting the ball from Jackie's grasp. Jack Matthews and Billy Cleaver were right on the spot, and in less time than it takes to tell I had received the vital pass and was racing upfield with the packed stand and terraces a bedlam of excitement around me.

It all happened so swiftly that the details are inevitably confused, but I can recall sensing, rather than actually seeing, the figure of George Norton looming ahead of me, and also hearing Malcolm Thomas as he called for the ball outside me. The pass, thank goodness, was timed and accurate. Malcolm then just threw his head back and went for the corner as though pursued by the combined forces of the Sinn Fein and I.R.A., finally reaching the line submerged in a blanket of green jerseys. For a horrible moment we thought that Malcolm had been tackled into touch, but to our heartfelt relief Mr Beattie signalled 'Try', and that was that.

Not quite, though, for the remaining few minutes were for me, and I'm sure the rest of the boys, quite the longest and nerve-racking I've ever endured on a rugger field. After what seemed an age the final whistle sounded, and the Ravenhill field became one huge patchwork of red and white as our ecstatic followers ran on to congratulate us.

Little did we know it, however, but the celebrations that attended Wales's first Triple Crown victory in forty years was in a matter of hours to turn into mourning over one of the worst air tragedies within memory - the Llandow disaster in which nearly a hundred rugby-loving Welsh men and women lost their lives.

* * * * *

With the Triple Crown and International Championship safely in the bag, all Welshmen now looked forward to a real grand finale against the French at Cardiff Arms Park, and for once at least they got it.

Conditions both overhead and underfoot were just perfect, and the boys responded with a magnificent display of open and spectacular rugby. We all, I think, enjoyed it immensely, for there was no longer the necessity to confine ourselves to the orthodox; indeed we just let ourselves go, with the result that the unfortunate French, deprived for much of the game of the services of the great Jean Prat, were virtually overwhelmed by the speed of our running and passing. The final margin was 21-0. Goal-kicking brought me nine of the points, to bring my tally up to seventeen in my first season of international rugby - needless to say, I was more than satisfied with it.

If the season had been a great one for me, it had been of even greater moment for Welsh rugby as a whole, and this I'm sure is as good a time as any to pay a tribute to some of the fine players I played alongside during our invincible season. First and foremost I must give my own special mention to Jack Matthews, whose power bursts and stout-hearted tackling were such important items in our success.

His footballing contribution apart, however, Jack was to

me at least one of the greatest morale boosters I have ever had the good fortune to play alongside. Not only was the solidity of his tackling an inspiration in itself, but in addition he frequently went out of his way to offer a word of encouragement and advice to young players who like myself were newcomers to the big-time stuff. Indeed, I cannot find words to define the vast inspiration and reassurance I received from Jackie in the course of the tough Triple Crown battles, particularly those at Twickenham and Ravenhill. It all makes a mockery of the silly rumours that were in circulation just after that 19-0 defeat at Murrayfield in 1951, rumours which alleged that Jackie and I had almost come to blows in the dressing-room after the game. Ignoring the fact that I am not in any case a 'fighting man', Jackie Matthews is the last man I would ever think of quarrelling with - I am far too grateful to him for the help and encouragement he gave me when I needed it most.

Other great heroes of the 1950 season were, of course, Ken Jones, who tackled unerringly and ran like a stag when opportunity presented itself, Malcolm Thomas, who put himself alongside Teddy Morgan and the other immortals with his try at Belfast, and Rex Willis, one of the pluckiest inside-halves I've ever played with. The real strong man behind our scrum though was Billy Cleaver, who played to a nicety the tactics that John Gwilliam demanded of him. Billy was in fact a natural footballer, and accordingly versatile enough to have fulfilled any role asked of him. What a boon players of his type are to any team, and touring teams in particular!

The real basis of our success, though, as has been claimed many times over, were our forwards, and in fact I very much doubt whether any of the Home Unions has at any time fielded a pack of forwards as rugged and mobile as this one.

I will never begin to agree with my friend Bleddyn

Williams's criticisms of John Gwilliam. He knew his own mind, and wasn't afraid to state it, and overall seemed to give you the impression that you were playing for him as much as for Wales. In particular he led the pack superbly, and by golly, he had some material to lead!

In the front row for instance was our pet humourist Cliff Davies, who, I'm afraid, did not strike our opponents as such, as he lent his every ounce of strength and energy to the fierce forward exchanges. Cliff, I'm convinced, would have been a riot in the Rugby League for he could run, pass, and handle a ball with the best of them. What a powerful and rugged customer too was Don Hayward, and what a wonderful jumper in the line-out Roy John who, oddly enough, would not even have been in the side at all if the selectors had had their way.

Greatest of the eight 'Red Devils' of 1950 was, in my mind, Ray Cale, who subsequently, of course, joined the St Helens club as a professional. Ray makes no secret of the fact that it was his disappointment at being unable to win a place in the British team tour to New Zealand and Australia that largely influenced his decision to turn pro - and I for one will hardly blame him. To my mind and, I'm sure, to the minds of the thousands who saw him in action between the years of 1948-50, Ray Cale was far and away the outstanding exponent of wing-forward play during this period, which means that any team leaving these shores without him could not be termed as 'fully representative' of the British Isles.

If my readers in the North are inclined to raise an eyebrow at this latter statement, then let me assure them that the Ray Cale who played for Wales in the Triple Crown season of 1950 was twice the player who later alternated between loose forward and the second row with St Helens. Certainly the Union game never treated this great Newbridge forward with the courtesy and gratitude to which he was entitled.

4

FOR THE NAVY AND THE BA-BAS

No young footballer could ever have achieved greater fame and distinction than that which had come my way during the fabulous winter of 1949-50, for truly everything I had touched in the rugby sense had seemed to turn to gold.

I had been lucky - incredibly so - for while many fine and worthy players had to my own knowledge striven seasons for the honour of representing their country but once, I, in a matter of months, had achieved almost every single honour open to a rugby player in Great Britain. I had played for my country, represented the Navy in the Inter-Services Tournament at Twickenham, and to my wildest delight been invited to accompany the Barbarians on their Easter time tour in South Wales.

It was all very gratifying for a youngster not yet nineteen. Indeed were it not for the blazers reposing new and imposing in my wardrobe back home, I would in all probability have expected to wake up one day and find it all a dream.

King of Rugger

My memories of that tremendous winter are of necessity confused, but there are several that stand out above the rest, one of them being that of the Army-Navy match at Twickenham. It was in this particular encounter that I kicked the penalty goal which some people have since claimed was one of the longest ever as regards distance. Mr. Vivian Jenkins of the *Sunday Times*, I notice, estimates the distance from kick to pitch as something like eighty yards, but what I feel will interest readers more than the actual feat itself is the story underlying it.

This starts with a major disaster - to the boots I had used throughout my first-class career until that match. At a practice on a London ground on the Friday before the big match, sole and upper parted company for the last time, with the result that I had to approach my father who was up in London for the match for the wherewithal to purchase another pair. Dad, I can tell you, was none too pleased with the request, for although he was always ready to help and encourage me in my games playing, he reasoned (not unjustly, I think) that in this particular instance the British Navy could well afford a small item such as this without jeopardizing in any way the defence of our shores.

In the end, however, he forked out the necessary, so the situation was saved, and I trotted out on Twickenham resplendent in a brand new pair of Cotton Oxfords.

Not that they had a very encouraging christening, for the Army XV on the day were rather too good for us, with the result that at half-time we faced a deficit of eleven points. Soon after half-time we were awarded a penalty on the touchline at half-way, and as our forwards were being subjected to something of a battering our skipper suggested that I 'should mess about with a shot at goal to give them a breather'. Thus it came about that the 'Wonder Goal' of the newspaper reports was in plain fact just another example of the way in which unrelated and apparently insignificant incidents can conspire to produce a headline.

Incidentally, Vivian Jenkins, who computed the length of my Twickenham goal, has always been my favourite rugby writer. He has, to begin with, always been kind to me, although I dare say the fact that I have played all my bad matches out of his ken largely accounts for this! Apart from this, though, I regard Vivian as the perfect example of the great player turned writer.

I do not claim of course that one has necessarily to have played rugby football to be able to write about it, but speaking as a player I find that both praise and censure are much more acceptable when they come from someone who has actually been in the middle themselves. From such persons a pat on the back really is an encouragement, and by the same token one is more ready to accept criticism when one knows it is backed by truly expert knowledge. Certainly few men could possess a wider knowledge of the game, its mode of conduct and background in different parts of the world, for during his wonderful career as the Welsh full-back during the mid-thirties, Vivian toured South Africa with a British representative team, whilst as a writer he has visited all the major rugby-playing countries.

Talking of tours and travelling immediately brings me back to one of the highlights of what was for me the wonderful winter of 1950 - the invitation to tour South Wales at Easter time with the famous Barbarians.

So much has been written about the Barbarian Club that its name is a household word throughout the Rugby Union world, and the honour of selection for one of the club tours is regarded by the lucky recipient as second only to the award of an international cap. For me, a mere lad not long out of school, the experience of my first tour was truly an unforgettable one. At the Esplanade Hotel, Penarth, which is the club's traditional H.Q., the atmosphere was nothing if not festive, and to glamorize the occasion still further there was I rubbing shoulders with some of the greatest names in rugby football, both past and present.

I played on three Easter tours for the Ba-Bas, but the first one will always remain outstanding in my memory; indeed as I shall recall later, there were incidents to mar the memory of at least one of them.

To begin with, this first Barbarian tour was in the nature of a triumphant home-coming to my own South Wales, for seldom have the 'gremlins' of rugby been more favourably disposed towards me. On the Cardiff Arms Park on Easter Saturday, for instance, I was fortunate enough to score all the points (two tries and a conversion) in an 8-6 victory over Cardiff, and then at Swansea had the privilege of being in at the kill when we played one of the most thrilling matches I've ever taken part in. With mere minutes to go Swansea were leading 11-6, and with their forwards storming inside our twenty-five, it looked as though we were booked for defeat. This was the moment, however, for the Ba-Bas to produce the brand of football for which they are famous; disdaining the consequences, our Army half-backs, Hardy and Shuttleworth, opened up from a scrum, full-back Murray Hoffmeyer swept into the line, and John Smith of Cambridge University was sent speeding for the line with every eye in that huge Bank Holiday crowd fixed upon him. The line must have looked a whole continent away to John as he began that lonely run, and for the whole pulsating length of it he had the covering Swansea defence racing frantically across field to cut him off. It has everything, that run of Smith's - speed, stamina, and fantastic determination - and as he grounded the ball beneath the St Helens' cross-bar the whole ground rose to him, and that included the players.

My conversion was almost an anti-climax, yet I was

pleased about it, for by saving the match it brought the just reward for John Smith's superb effort. He always impressed me as a great wing three-quarter, did John Smith, and I can never accordingly account for his rather abrupt disappearance from the game.

The last match of this memorable tour was at Rodney Parade, Newport, and coincided with my nineteenth birthday - April 11th - and once again John Smith brought the house down with one of his specials. This time, though, we were defeated, but that in no way detracted from my satisfaction over what had been a fine rousing game, and as such a grande finale to a wonderful tour.

Earlier on I referred to an incident that marred the memory of my third and final tour with the Ba-Bas, but only as the final answer to the many different versions that have been in circulation ever since the Easter Tuesday afternoon at Newport when it was found that my name had been withdrawn from the Barbarian team at the last moment. The common version is that I had got into hot water with the Barbarian authorities for contravening regulations and had accordingly been sent home in disgrace.

Needless to relate, there are several supplementary anecdotes to explain just how I did contravene regulations. Well, the true facts are, as always, fairly simple. I had played for the team at Penarth on the Good Friday, and also at Swansea on the Easter Monday, which meant of course that according to custom I would not be required to play at Newport in the last game of the tour on the Tuesday. It seems, however, that Newport had contacted the Ba-Bas on the possibility of my turning out as a boost to the holiday gate at Rodney Parade, and when the subject was broached to me personally I readily agreed, for I would rather play a game of rugger than watch from the stand any day. So far so good, then.

King of Rugger

I played at Swansea, and then on Cardiff station on the way back to Penarth I bumped into Frank Fenner, a colleague of mine in the Devonport Services team, who had been touring with the Services in South Wales. Frank had lost his connection back to barracks and was accordingly about to go in search of a hotel for the night. On learning this I had a brain-wave - a misguided one, as I realise now - and suggested he take my room at the Esplanade at Penarth, while I would stay the night at my fiancée's parents. This was readily acceptable to Frank, and even more so to myself, but not alas to the Barbarian officials, for on Tuesday morning when I reported to the Esplanade in readiness for the Newport match I was met (appropriately, I'm sure) on the mat by one of the officials, who there and then proceeded to give me a real dressing-down for my absence from the hotel the night before.

I said nothing, for deep down I knew I deserved it, but when he ended his observations with the comment, 'I've got a good mind to leave you out of the side at Newport this afternoon,' I got rather nettled, for after all I had been asked specially to play although it was my turn to rest. Anyway, to curtail the agony, I about faced and told the official that the 'wish was father to the thought', and straight away left for my home at Gorseinon.

Those then are the facts of the much-publicized Barbarian incident, and as I say, I take most of the blame for, if nothing else, a great deal of thoughtlessness; however, even now, and in possession of whatever additional wisdom I've accumulated in the intervening years, I cannot see that my offence was as heinous as all that, and I would still, I think, resent the kind of words used by the official on that altogether regrettable occasion.

Indeed, this was not the only occasion I got into hot water with the Ba-Ba authorities, for I believe it was on the same tour that I decided at the last moment to utilize my rest day by playing for Llanelly. Time was short, and transport too, the only form readily available being Malcolm Thomas's fiery two-stroke motor-cycle. Not, I suspect, without misgivings, Malcolm signified consent, and away I roared, or rather two-stroked, in the direction of Llanelly. I didn't two-stroke smoothly, however, for every couple of miles the plug kept oiling up, so by the time I reached my home town at Gorseinon time was running desperately short.

There was time for but one call, and that an essential one, on my old pal Roy Warlow, the 'Motor Bike King of all Llwchr'. In no time at all Roy had fixed the 'phuts' in my (or Malcolm's) cylinder head, and I eventually reached Stradey just as the teams were leaving the dressing-rooms. Sportingly, the chap who had been chosen to play in my place stood down for me, but on reflection I was a thoroughly bad sport to let him. I wouldn't think of it nowadays, anyhow, but then I suppose one is pretty thoughtless when one is young.

After the match I spent an hour or two at home, and then set out back for Penarth where I was due to play in the Barbarian Golf Competition on the Sunday morning. As dusk approached, however, and I switched on the lights, I found to my horror that there weren't any. For a minute or two I toyed with the idea of chancing my luck, but on second thoughts decided that I had already used up my allotted portion of good luck for the day by being allowed to travel fifty odd miles unmolested for the motor-cycle licence I didn't possess. I therefore turned back for home, and if, when I reported at Penarth some time after midday on the Sunday, my reception wasn't exactly frigid, neither was it obviously a warm one.

In retrospect I feel that neither of these incidents particularly endeared me to those in charge of this very famous touring team, and I feel that they may also have helped to give the impression that I was a difficult customer to handle, an impression which seems, to a certain degree at least, to have stuck down the years. What am I to answer to that? Well, goodness knows it's difficult to be self-analytical at any time, more so when you can pick up the newspaper on most days of the week and read what a dozen other people think of you. All I can say is this: I may have been thoughtless, especially so when I was a teenager. I may have made a remark or two off the cuff without thinking about their possible interpretation, and I may occasionally have displeased those who consider it the duty of a paid entertainer to carry his entertaining into the social world of club and pub, but in all sincerity I have never set out to be deliberately rude to anyone.

Someone indeed once described me as 'a nearly inarticulate product of the Welsh hills'! I hope I am not quite that, but then neither am I particularly fluent at expressing in words my appreciation and gratitude to the many people and organizations amongst whom, and in many cases by whose direct assistance, I have so enjoyed my rugby career, whether amateur or professional. Is it this latter, I wonder, that sometimes arouses misunderstanding?

5

TO NEW ZEALAND

For me at least rugby football for the 1949-50 season ended with the completion of the Barbarians Easter tour in South Wales, and I returned to Devonport looking forward to a summer on the cricket field.

In the meantime the British Lions party, led by Karl Mullen, had sailed for Australasia, and although some of the newspaper critics opined that I should have been amongst them I was not, to be perfectly frank, all that disappointed. True, I experienced a twinge of envy at the thought of Malcolm and the rest of the fellows I had got to know travelling to places I had only read about, but then I contented myself with the reflection that I was after all only nineteen and, moreover, had not done so badly in the space of a few brief months in first-class football.

It was pleasant anyway to be enjoying my first taste of all-day cricket, having previously only played Saturday-afternoon stuff.

King of Rugger

Certainly rugby football was far from my mind on the June afternoon I was playing for the United Services XI in a match at the Mount Wise ground, Plymouth. It was during the luncheon interval, I think, that I was called to the telephone to speak to that great Barbarian personality (now alas departed), Mr H.A. Haigh-Smith, who told me that it looked as though I might be required to fly out to New Zealand as a replacement for the Irish full-back George Norton, who had broken an arm some weeks earlier.

I could hardly believe Mr Haigh-Smith, whom I can still hear to this day chuckling at my own incredulity. Sure enough, later in the afternoon came the confirmatory telegram from the Secretary of the Rugby Union, informing me that I was required to fly from London Airport on June 17th (exactly a week later) to join the party who would be at Gisborne in the North Island of New Zealand.

Looking at a cutting in my scrap-book, I find that I scored sixty runs for the Services on the afternoon of my selection; I have to accept the report, for quite honestly I don't remember a single incident of that particular cricket match as I could think of nothing else but the wonderful news I had received from London.

The next few days were a whirl of feverish activity - the hurried journey home to South Wales, the hectic shopping expeditions in Swansea, and finally, of course, the wonderful send-off at Swansea High Street station from my family and friends. Though, as I say, I inevitably forget the details, I shall never forget the wonderful kindness extended to me by the sports-loving people of Gorseinon who saw to it -and most handsomely - that I should not miss my opportunity for any financial reason. Indeed if ever I play cricket again for Gorseinon, as I hope to do some day, then I shall owe them an awful lot of runs to make up for the kindness the village folk showed me then.

To see me off at the Airport was my brother Cliff, and soon I was airborne on the B.O.A.C. Stratocruiser *Speedbird*, *en route* for the greatest adventure of all.

This is not a travel book, so I'll spare you the description of my awe and wonder as we passed over, and sometimes alighted at, such places as Gander, Shannon, Honolulu, and New York, places I had previously only known as names in the geography books back at Gowerton School. Finally I arrived at Whenupai Airport in Auckland two days after I had set out from London, and was met there by Mr F.E. Sutherland, the President of the Auckland Rugby Union, and another prominent provincial administrator, Mr G. Orrell.

Later at my hotel my feeling of strangeness, together with the first pangs of home sickness, were vastly relieved by a conversation with Mervyn Corner, who had himself visited Wales as a member of the All Black side in 1935. Then later in the day I flew on to Gisborne where the British party were assembled in readiness for their match with the combined Poverty Bay, East Coast, and Bay of Plenty XV, which was to take place three days later. Believe you me, after the long flight and arrival in an absolutely strange country, it was good to see again faces I knew, particularly those of the Welsh contingent!

Rather to my surprise I found myself in the side for the Gisborne match, which much to my relief turned out an easy one for us. We won 27-3, my own tally being three conversions. Those details I've had to check on, since what I actually remember is a stunning display by Jack Matthews, and the spectacle of Scotland's front-row forward Don Budge tearing down the wing like an outsize edition of Ken Jones.

From Gisborne we travelled down to Wellington at the tip of the North Island for two of the important matches of the tour, those with the strong Wellington Provincial side, and the Third Test match against New Zealand. Rightly, in view of the fact that I was so short of match practice, I was not included for either game, so I was able to sit in the stand of the famous Athletic Ground and enjoy the spectacle of Bleddyn Williams at his peerless best. What a spectacle it was, for the famous 'jink' flashed in and out like a neon sign, to blind the Wellington players with its brilliance. Bleddyn scored two great tries, and the huge crowd of 30,000, which included that renowned enthusiast, Sir Bernard Freyburg, v.c., must have enjoyed it all immensely.

A week later, during which I had thoroughly imbibed and likewise enjoyed the atmosphere of tremendous enthusiasm the New Zealanders generate over rugby matters, I was again a spectator in the Wellington stand, this time, however, to see our lads go down to New Zealand by six points to three.

This was my first view of the famous All Blacks in action, and what impressed me most was the terrific fervour and ferocity of their giant forwards. Even when injuries had reduced their number to six, they never let up their efforts plus that of the crippled centre three-quarter Elvidge, who ran like a hero for the winning try, most certainly carrying the day for New Zealand.

As I say, I admired intensely both the spirit and the disciplined unity of New Zealand forward play, yet as I thought then, and indeed still think, it would not do Rugby Union football any good were the methods adopted by All Black packs in their own country to become general in the rest of the rugby world. 'Everything above grass, boys' is a phrase often used by pack leaders the world over, but nowhere is it interpreted quite so literally as in New Zealand.

There are sufficient risks attached to the playing of rugby football without adding to them by licensing the game to become more hacking matches. I am, I consider, being sensible rather than squeamish, and in any case, both by natural aptitude and physique, New Zealand forwards strike me as being well-equipped to measure against the world's best without resorting to methods of so primitive and physically dangerous a character. For the rest of New Zealand rugby I have nothing but intense admiration, containing as it does many features which could profitably be emulated in this country.

From Wellington then on to Wanganui where I had my fist view of the world-famous 'Haka', the war dance with which New Zealand sides in Britain delight or, according to temperament, awe the opposition before a big match. In this case, of course, the atmosphere of the 'Haka' was all the more awe-inspiring, since it was actually performed by the Maori tribesmen of the Wanganui River. Presumably, however, the lads were inured to the performance by now, for we fairly romped home to a 31-3 victory, which afforded me immense satisfaction for, as seven 'bulls' out of seven attempts signified, it showed that my goal-kicking had not suffered as the result of the rather brusque transportation from England to New Zealand.

Three days later we were at New Plymouth to meet those redoubtable Ranfurly Shield fighters, Taranaki - the province which, as an older generation of followers in Britain will be interested to learn, produced that super player of Dave Gallaher's original All Blacks, Johnny Hunter.

Since Taranaki were renowned for the power of their forward play we expected a hard match against them, but with Jackie Kyle at his devastating best we won easily once more, this time by twenty-five points to three. Taranaki incidentally was the scene of Bill McKay's epic encounter with the wildest of pigs.

King of Rugger

Thanks to the kindness of our farming hosts, Mr and Mrs R.W. Larsen of Uruti, Bill, Gordon Rimmer, John Robins and myself were taken on a pig-hunting expedition during which a large and obviously irate sow came charging down on McKay, who was for the moment weaponless. Seeing his predicament the experienced members of the party urged him to 'jump on its back'! No sooner urged than done, and there was the sow careering madly into the undergrowth with the big Irish forward clinging grimly to its flanks. It was certainly no joke for Bill, but the rest of us were in fits of mirth; fortunately the rider (!) held tight, and the animal was finally secured and dispatched, much to the relief of even so intrepid a character as Bill McKay.

On from New Plymouth to Palmerston North where the side, without me this time (but not because of it), made heavy weather of defeating Manawatu Horowhenua, and then to Hamilton where, incidentally, rugby in New Zealand was first played. At Hamilton we met another combined XV, this time the representatives of the Unions of Waikato, King Country, and Thames Valley, and once again the boys played brilliantly to win 30-0.

A match with North Auckland (8-6 to us) intervening, we finally arrived at the world-famous Eden Park Stadium, Auckland, where we met the Auckland Provincial side as a full-dress rehearsal for the Fourth and Final Test match a week ahead.

Eden Park, where the Empire Games had been held a year previously, is, with its vast terraces, a stadium to tug strongly on both the memory and the imagination. I most certainly will remember it even when I am an old man telling hugely embellished tales to my grandchildren. With Twickenham, and the Wooloongabba ground at Brisbane, Australia, Eden Park was the scene of my greatest triumph in rugby football.

Naturally I was more than a little nervous as I trooped out behind Karl Mullen to face the vast sea of faces on the cram-packed terraces of this famous ground on Saturday, July 22nd, 1950. And with good reason, for Auckland were one of the strongest provincial sides in New Zealand, whilst even more foreboding from my point was the fact that they had at full-back none other than the great Bob Scott who, as I'd been told over and over again in New Zealand, was the very greatest of them all.

It was a glorious afternoon for rugby, summer-like, in fact, and with the sun in his eyes Bob Scott badly misjudged my kick-off, which, as always, was a long, boring effort right down into the opponent's twenty-five. Possibly the fact that I had found Scott as fallible as other mortals encouraged me; whatever the reason, I found top form right from the start, and found moreover little difficulty in holding Bob in our duels down the touchline.

The Lions took the lead with a try by Bill McKay, only for Auckland to first equalize and then take the lead with a penalty goal by Scott, and a try from Crowley. Then with half-time approaching Auckland were penalised on the half-way line near touch, and as soon as my boot hit the ball I knew it was a goal. As the ball soared high above the cross-bar I knew too that this was going to be my day.

Sometimes you feel these things in your bones even before you touch a ball, and this was just such an occasion; looking back on my career I cannot recall that things ever went better or more effortlessly for me than on Eden Park that afternoon. When the end came we had piled up thirty-two points to Auckland's nine, my own personal tally being seventeen (four conversions, and three penalty goals). Even so, the day belonged to Jackie Kyle, for the great little Irish stand-off half played one of the most wonderful matches I have ever seen him play, and that despite being badly kicked about at the feet of the Province forwards. I've seen some 'dirty' play in my time, but nothing so completely ruthless and deliberate as the kicking of Jackie on the ground right in front of the grandstand at Eden Park that afternoon.

Seven days later we were back at the stadium again, amid an atmosphere of tension and excitement that was even greater than on the first occasion. New Zealand had of course already won the 'rubber', but that detracted nothing from the magnitude of the occasion; on the contrary, the brand of attacking rugger we had produced at Eden Park the previous Saturday had unmistakably whetted the appetites of the huge crowd which had been flocking into the ground since early morning. Some of them, in fact, had arrived complete with thermos flasks and blankets to camp outside the gates the previous evening, and for miles around the ground on the afternoon of the match the sunlight flashed and glinted on the windscreens of the cars, parked in every conceivable cranny and cul-de-sac.

Even my no-so-distant January memory of Twickenham faded before this scene, with its attendant noise that was quite fantastic as we lined up before our rather grim-looking opponents in their all-black outfits. The line-up for those who like their statistics in order was as follows.

Great Britain: Lewis Jones, Ken Jones, Jack Matthews, B.L. Williams, M. Lane, Jack Kyle, Rex Willis, R.T. Evans, J.M. McKay, P. Kinninmonth, Roy John, J.D. Nelson, Cliff Davies, D.M. Davies, D.Budge.

New Zealand: R.W.H. Scott, Peter Henderson, W.A. Meates, R.A. Roper, J. Tanner, L.S. Haig, Vince Bevan, P. Johnstone, R.A.White, L.R. Harvey, P.Crowley, A.M. Hughes, K. Skinner, H. Wilson, E. Mexted.

Of the New Zealand team that day, Scott, Tanner, Haig, Bevan, R.A. 'Snow' White, and Kevin Skinner all became even more well known to British followers as members of the All Blacks party of 1953, whilst Peter Henderson, who is these days a very good friend of mine, subsequently endeared himself to Rugby League fans in the North of England as as free-scoring three-quarter with Huddersfield.

Back then to Eden Park, July 29th, 1950, and a struggle as thrilling as any I can remember. For once in a while the genius of Jack Kyle was largely subdued by the first-time tackling of his opposite number, Haig of Otago - a stopper pure and simple if ever there was one. Poor Rex Willis too was taking the father and mother of a lacing from Pat Crowley on the blind side of the scrum, and what with the usual ferocious rucking tactics of the New Zealand pack as whole, there did not seem much future for the Lions at Eden Park that afternoon. Bleddyn and Jack were of course having a real go at it in the centre, and our forwards were also sticking to their task magnificently, but up to ten minutes from time the All Blacks, with a lead of 11-3, looked quite safely home. Then it happened - a scrum went down almost on our goal-line, Rex flicked a beauty out to Kyle who shaped to pass to Bleddyn.

In a flash I saw the gap, and a the New Zealand centres fanned out to engage Bleddyn, I sped between, took the ball from Kyle, and galloped up past the half-way line where Ken Jones, fine anticipatory player that he is, was right at my elbow. Having drawn Bob Scott to the point where he was committed to a tackle I switched the ball to Ken, who went for the Eden Park goal-line as only he can. He had something like forty yards to go and Peter Henderson who chased him was no slouch, yet every yard Ken ran seemed to pull him further away as though on some invisible elastic band. I kicked the goal without difficulty, and the crowd were roaring now, for they sensed that we might pull the game off.

Truly I'll never forget the dying moments of that match, for as Kyle, Bleddyn, and Jackie Matthews threw all they had in an endeavour to pull the game out of the fire, the 60,000 present fairly rose to them, as though, in fact they were trying to do it for New Zealand. Minutes from time, and after a succession of wonderful back movements, Ireland's Mick Lane was hauled down on the corner flag after a breath-taking run - and that for us was the last shot in the locker. We had failed, but gloriously, and the crowd knew it. How they cheered us as we made for the dressing-rooms, and how sweet and plaintively too did the strains of 'Now is the Hour' sound in that vast stadium. It was almost like being back again on the Arms Park, and for us Welshmen especially it was a link with far-off-home - so real as to bring a lump to the throat.

6

RUGBY IN WALLABY LAND

All that remained now after the epic of Eden Park were the
farewells to the so friendly islands of New Zealand, and
once again the scene was sad and intensely emotional as we
waved our last farewells from the deck of the liner
Wanganella as the crowds massing the wharf at Dunedin
sang the songs we had come to love so well.

Then on to Australia, and after a pipe-opener at Canberra
against a New South Wales Country XV, whom we defeated
easily, the Lions arrived at Sydney where we expected a stiff
tussle with the New South Wales State team, which is
virtually representative of the full strength Australian rugby.

If we had but known it, however, New South Wales
rugby was in a transitionary period, for many of the fine
players who had accompanied the Wallabies to Britain two
years earlier had retired and the Selectors were being hard
pressed to fill the gaps. Trevor Allen too was unable to turn
out owing to injury, so that with one thing and another we

were able to win with less trouble than we had anticipated. The margin in fact was 22-6, and the most outstanding feature the fine play of Rhys Stephens, who had been so unlucky with injuries on the New Zealand part of the tour.

After the State match followed the long trip to Queensland for the First Test with Australia on the famous Wooloongabba Ground at Brisbane. The name 'Wooloongabba' figures prominently in this book, and you need hardly ask why, for it is on this ground, where Australia stages Test cricket and rugby football under both League and Union codes, that I was fortunate enough to establish world records under either code.

In 1950, and under Union rules, I scored sixteen points (a try, drop goal, two penalty goals, and two conversions) to beat the individual scoring record for internationals established by 'Ockey' Geffin for South Africa against New Zealand at Johannesburg a year earlier, 'Ockey's' tally being fifteen, all penalties. Then on the same ground, four years later, this time as a member of the British Rugby League side led by my compatriot Dickie Williams, I kicked ten goals against Australia to break the Rugby League record of nineteen points only recently established by the Australian player Noel Pidding.

The 'Gabba', my own connection with it notwithstanding, is in other respects an odd sporting arena. The rugby players for instance actually play on the cricket square where Test matches are played barely months later; then there are the torrential tropical rainstorms that in a matter of minutes can transform a sports arena into a lake, in the majority of cases (as history has proved) to the detriment of the English batsmen who have had to bat last on typical Brisbane 'Sticky Dogs'. Cricketers pale at the mere prospect. Still, you won't find me criticizing the 'Gabba', on the contrary I'd like to carry it around with me wherever I play!

As far as the First Test of 1950 went, the Lions were much too good for Australia. To begin with our forwards, supported adroitly by Jack Kyle with his touch-kicking, gave them the full 'Test treatment'. Indeed, the Brisbane crowd liked these tactics a good deal less even than the Australian players and booed incessantly as we kicked for the line as part of the preliminary softening-up process. I don't blame them either, for this so-called 'Test rugby' with its concentration on close forward play and kicking by the backs is even more boring to watch than it is to play. Besides, not even in Rugby Union is direct kicking to touch permitted in the ordinary club match in Australia, so the spectators have a legitimate grouse when under the Rugby Union rules, it is employed in an international.

For my own part I cannot see why the dispensation as regards kicking to touch, which the Rugby Union have allowed the Australians, could not be extended to operate in full internationals. That to my mind at least is only logical or why allow the Aussies to alter the rules of Rugby Union in the first place? Reverting again to the Brisbane match, once the Australians had been rattled by our initial tactics, the way was open for the backs, and with Jack Kyle creating wide gaps in midfield, Jack Matthews and Bleddyn had one of their field days.

A week later we were back at Sydney for the Second Test, and once again we carried too many guns for the Aussies, even though they were reinforced this time by those fine players, Trevor Allen and Arthur Tonkin. The margin this time was 24-3, and as at Brisbane our stronger and more tactically applied forward play made the vital difference. Before leaving for home, however, we came a real cropper at Newcastle, which is a name of ill omen particularly for Rugby League touring teams. There we were defeated 12-17 by a New South Wales XV which contained many of the players who had played against us in the two previous Tests and State games. I had a poor match at Newcastle, and so too, though more excusably, did others in the team who were now beginning to feel the effects of a long and arduous tour.

It had been a wonderful experience, but none of us were, I think, sorry when we finally docked at Tilbury after calling in at Ceylon to play a match on the homeward voyage. The going for the majority of the team had become appreciably harder as the tour neared its end. My own personal record on the tour (including the match at Ceylon) was 114 points in seven matches in New Zealand, and six in Australia, but from a goal-kicking viewpoint I'm sure that the real hero of the tour had been my great friend Malcolm Thomas, who revealed one more aspect of his magnificent versatility by turning himself into a place-kicker, and a successful one too, at the behest of his harassed captain. So well indeed did Malcolm step into the breach caused by the injury of George Norton that for strictly official purposes he was the team's leading scorer with nine tries, eighteen conversions, and eleven penalty goals - ninety-six points in all. This was a magnificent achievement for a player who had seldom been given an opportunity to try at goal back in Britain.

Malcolm had developed a place-kicking technique of his own, and he was kind enough to pass the tip on to me when he had found it effective. His method, which of course applied to conversions, was to dig an extraordinary large hole in the ground, and then get his placer to lower the ball in with the back of the hands showing to the opposition lined up behind their posts. This was the key to the whole business, for the placer's hands were adjusted over the ball in such a way as to conceal the fact that the ball was well and truly down from the moment the ball was in the hole. The holding, in effect, was all bluff, and it goes without saying that I was highly impressed with both the results achieved by Malcolm and the possibilities of its adaptation to my own use. Alas, and much I don't doubt, to my detriment I never had the cheek to try it in an actual match. On the few occasions I even toyed with the idea I always had the feeling that the referee was looking extra hard at me as I was walking up to take the kick. I can only hope that this disclosure does not get Malcolm into hot water with referees - retrospective as it is.

Of the many great players I played with and against on this my first major tour, I would award the palm to Ireland's Jack Kyle, who on his form in Australia and, particularly, in New Zealand, was easily the greatest stand-off half whom I, at least, have ever seen in any class of football, League or Union.

The perfect player is of course only the dream of the theorist or hero worshipper, but Kyle on his Australasian form was very nearly two footballers in one - the brilliant attacker, and the stout and shrewd defender. He had to be seen to be believed, which means that those who saw him in action out there will always believe him to be one of the greatest natural footballers who ever laced a boot. Bleddyn Williams and Jackie Matthews too enjoyed wonderful tours, and either, on that form, would go automatically into any World XV that I picked.

Ken Jones was another who captivated the crowds wherever he played, and no wonder, for of all the spectacles rugby football has to unfold, there is surely none more thrilling than that of the graceful Newport flier streaking linewards with a more than average chance of getting there. Spectators Down Under saw this spectacle a good deal more frequently than followers in this country, so is it any wonder that they raved over it?

As regards the 'enemy' I, like many another, quite

obviously came under the spell of New Zealand's Bob Scott, for he was a truly great player. Yet even as far back as 1950 when I first saw him, Bob was, to my mind, slightly over the hill, and he did in fact retire at the conclusion of the 1950 Test series. That is no depreciation of Scott's uncanny ability, on the contrary it is a recognition of what a superb player he must have been during the years that were wasted by war. He was a great full-back when I saw him, but there were times - and I used to watch him closely - when his concentration seemed to flag, especially when goal-kicking. I criticize, I know, on a very high plane, but then I'm trying to make my own personal assessment of a very fine player.

It was evident that New Zealand, despite her supremacy in the Tests, had no midfield backs to match, much less surpass, people like Kyle, Matthews, and Bleddyn Williams, and that I suppose was the inevitable result of their over-concentration on forward play. Fine forwards they had in plenty, and in this respect R.A.'Snow' White and Kevin Skinner were as good as I've seen in any company.

I've discussed New Zealand forward methods in another context, and accordingly I was not surprised that their meetings with the Springboks in 1955 should erupt in outbursts of rough, violent, and otherwise regrettable incidents.

Personally I see no fun either for player or spectator in this highly complicated business of making the game of rugby football a tactical exercise between two packs of forwards. The forwards have an important part in the game, but so have the backs, and I'm sure that great rugby, rugby that is as attractive to watch as well as play, can only be forthcoming when the balance of power is poised as near equally as possible between the two.

7

DISASTER AT MURRAYFIELD

A terrific welcome awaited the returning Lions, crowds met us at every railway station on the journey from London down to Wales, we were feted everywhere, and every village organized a tribute to its own representative.

As always Gorseinon did me proud, for at a civic reception at the Council Chamber I was presented with a vellum address by the Council Chairman, Mr T. Ivor Davies, whilst the rugby club organized a dinner in my honour at which I was presented with a fountain pen. That indeed was quite an occasion, for including myself, five Gorseinon internationals received presentations that evening, the others being Onllwyn Brace and Owen 'Fuser' Hughes, who had won secondary school caps, and Tony John and J.W. Davies, who had won similar honours with the Welsh Youth Rugby Union.

It had been a wonderful homecoming in every sense, but I think the greatest thrill of all was to play rugger once again for Gorseinon before my own folk.

King of Rugger

The match in which I played had been arranged as part of the 'welcome home' party, and for the occasion that fine Swansea forward and even finer sportsman, Bryn Evans, had brought along an International XV to play the village club. And what a match it proved to be, for with Tony John throwing out a streamlined service our backs actually played more brilliantly than the internationals arrayed against them, to enable us to win 13-3.

They were hectic weeks, those first weeks of homecoming, for in addition to the social round the services of the Lions were in constant demand on the rugger field, with their clubs naturally enough anxious to have them in action again. Then there were the 'special' matches to be played. At Cardiff Arms Park, for instance, the Lions met Cardiff as part of the club's 75th anniversary celebrations, and at Landsdowne Road, Dublin, we played an Old Belvedere Select XV as an acknowledgement of Ireland's contribution to the tour. I'm glad to say that on both occasions the rugby was as memorable as the occasion that prompted it.

There was at the time much criticism of the demands made on the returning Lions, and in fact the belief still persists in many quarters that the Welsh debacle at Murrayfield a few months later was the direct outcome of the heavy demands made on the Lions contingent immediately upon their return. Personally I feel that is stretching things a little, for only a fortnight before the same XV had played brilliantly to defeat England at Swansea, and there was then certainly no hint of staleness in their performance. However there is no doubt that a long tour does produce a delayed reaction on the participants. This, I think, is not so much physical (after all, at twenty-five a player should be at peak fitness) as mental, for a tour is in more sense than one carried on in an atmosphere of perpetual climax. As a result, things seem to fall rather flat on one's return to the familiar environment. The incentive just is not there any more; in fact, after the tense excitement of Test matches abroad, even an international becomes 'just another game of football', and only a complete rest can get you keyed up once more. That, anyhow, is my answer to this much-debated point.

In any case I was luckier than the rest of the Welsh contingent, for after a short leave I was due back at Devonport where, as I mentioned earlier, the tempo of rugby is not nearly so intense as it is in South Wales. Thus my reorientation was much less strenuous than that of my fellow Welshmen who had been on the tour.

Incidentally a most pleasant surprise awaited me back at the Rectory ground - a surprise in the form of a beautiful cigarette box, presented to me by Rear-Admiral P.S. Smith, 'in (as the inscription related) recognition of his truly wonderful achievements in 1950 - Royal Navy, Barbarians, Wales, British Isles Touring Team'. It was a magnificent present, and a useful one too, for professional or not, I am not one of those who believe that a cigarette is a handicap to physical fitness.

With the exception of a broken finger sustained during a match with Barnstaple my rugby proceeded uneventfully up to the Christmas of 1950, but then of course things began to hot up as the first international with England at Swansea drew nearer. A game for Llanelly over the holiday helped me to re-acclimatize myself to the Welsh atmosphere, and the final Welsh Trial at Cardiff a few days later in which I played as a centre three-quarter reassured me that my form had not slipped, and even more important, that Wales seemed booked for another successful winter. With the exception of Ray Cale, who had turned pro, and Billy Cleaver, who had retired, the Triple Crown side was more or less intact; indeed there were many who contended that the inclusion of Glyn Davies at outside-half would actually strengthen the side from an attacking viewpoint, and as things turned out the

King of Rugger

match at St Helens, Swansea, seemed to confirm this opinion.

We began, in fact, exactly where we'd left off against France at the Arms Park the previous March, with a veritable carnival of grand open football.

For the first quarter of an hour or so our forwards kept the ball close in accordance with the Gwilliam's probing tactics, and then, with the situation sized up, let it loose to the backs who fairly ripped the English defence to pieces with the speed and unexpectedness of their manoeuvres. With Glyn Davies repeatedly slipping the England back row, Jack Matthews and I had the time of our lives in the centre, Malcolm Thomas and Ken Jones on the wings benefiting accordingly. The final score of 23-5, reflecting the biggest Welsh victory over England in thirty years, had the crowd beside themselves with delight.

As we in the Welsh XV preened ourselves over the weekend, the newspapers announced the beginning of a new 'Golden Era' for Welsh rugby. How easy it is to deceive oneself in rugby; certainly we kidded ourselves over the England match at Swansea. It was true that we backs in particular had played some brilliant rugby, but so delighted were we with our success that we completely ignored the fact that this was without a doubt one of the weakest England teams on record. Their defence in midfield was to all intents and purposes non-existent, and then I don't think a weaker back row than England's that afternoon has ever appeared on an international field in post-war years. An easy victory, too, had blinded a lot of people to certain weaknesses in our own team, for if nothing else, it should have been plain that our pack were not quite the force they had been the previous winter. This might smack of being wise after the event, yet I still insist that for the far-seeing, anyhow, the shadow of coming events was pretty accurately outlined on the turf of St Helens.

Be this as it may, however, the Welsh party, accompanied

by thousands of supporters, made the journey to Edinburgh in a mood of high confidence. Gorseinon needless to say were out in force for the occasion, and the village added its own bit of history to an historic occasion with a strictly Welsh version of the 'Stone of Scone' which a couple of intensely patriotic Scotsmen had recently appropriated from its resting-place in Westminster Abbey.

Headed by a pal of mine, Gordon Deeley, a former Swansea and Hull Kingston Rovers three-quarter, the 'sparks' of the village had conceived the novel idea of making a replica of the Coronation Chair, with the Stone (which lies underneath) fashioned out of a lump of Welsh anthracite. The boys had made a splendid job of this, which attracted considerable interest in the National Press at the time. Alas that it eventually, like our Triple Crown aspirations, became Scottish property! Today the model rests in an Edinburgh museum, where, as it was unkindly suggested at the time, most of the Welsh XV properly belonged - stuffed at that!

Before the match, however, there was no hint of what was to come. With one change (Alan Forward for Peter Evans at wing-forward) from the side that had so easily defeated England, we ran out to a roar that must assuredly have been heard back in Princes Street. Murrayfield is another of those grounds with an atmosphere, an atmosphere that can only be described as obviously hostile to all things not Scottish! Wales, it goes without saying, had any number of supporters high up on those packed terraces, but it was noticeable that whenever the Murrayfield roar assumed really deafening proportions, it was always the Scots who were threatening.

As usual Gwilliam urged his forwards in for the preliminary onslaught, and for a while the situation seemed well in hand with our forwards apparently getting the ball back fairly regularly from the scrums, even though a trifle sluggishly. Our backs, certainly, were more frequently in action than Scotland's in the opening period, but nevertheless it was an ominous sign that the Scottish forwards were not wilting before our own pack as others had done in the Triple Crown campaign of the previous season. The Scottish back row, and Elliott in particular, found the slow heeling very much to their advantage, with result that Glyn Davies, Jack Matthews, and myself were soon receiving something of a shellacking in midfield.

Even when half-time came with Scotland a penalty goal to the good, we were by no means disheartened for we reckoned that the Welsh side as a whole still had a bit in reserve for the real testing period ahead. There I think you have, from a Welsh viewpoint, the whole sad story of Murrayfield, for when Gwilliam early in the second half mustered his forwards for a really full-scale onslaught, they found that the Scottish forwards could take it all and some more on top. The discovery, I'm certain, caused discouragement in the Welsh pack, and by the same token a mounting confidence in the Scots, who now began to play with terrific verve and fury.

Perhaps you could liken that Scottish pack to a prize fighter who, having taken the best his opponent could throw at him, suddenly realizes that he cannot be hurt, and therefore sails in regardless, with both fists going like windmills. I once read an account of the Archie Moore-Marciano fight written by Peter Wilson in which the latter was asked the question, 'Why couldn't Moore with all his experience, skill, and ringcraft keep out of the way of Marciano's wild swings?' Wilson's answer was, 'Because it was like being in the ring with a run-away truck!' That I consider a fair enough description of what Elliott and his seven blue dervishes did to us at Murrayfield on that bitterly remembered February afternoon of 1951.

To blame (as has been done) Gwilliam's captaincy is both unfair and futile, for on the afternoon's play the Scottish forwards would have devoured any opposition. The full story has been written often enough to be common knowledge to both present and future generations of rugger followers - the Scottish forwards ran amok, Peter Kininmonth dropped a goal (to my knowledge the only one he ever tried in international football, much less kicked) to destroy the last remnants of our confidence, and then finally the whole Scottish side, both backs and forwards, surged through to score three more tries, leaving us unbelievably the vanquished by nineteen points to nil.

Inevitably there was a 'coroner's inquest' in every pub and factory in Welsh Wales, and there were indeed some pretty rum findings at some of them. It was alleged, for instance, that the eve of Murrayfield had been, as far as the Welsh players were concerned, like the eve of Waterloo, an occasion of wine, women and song. It was rumoured too that there had been friction between individual players which had culminated in blows in the dressing-rooms afterwards. What absolute nonsense! I can assure readers that the only truth in these rumours was that referring to song! We did indeed sing at our headquarters, the North British Hotel, before the match, as (you can take it from me) we did afterwards - and far into the night!

When the time came for the official inquest, held at the Royal Hotel, Cardiff, by the five members of the W.R.U. selection committee, it was discovered that the men mainly responsible for the Murrayfield disaster were Glyn Davies and myself amongst the backs, and Captain John Gwilliam of the forwards. For his sin John was relieved of the captaincy although he was still retained in the side, whilst Glyn and I were dropped outright. During the intervening years I have many times been asked how I felt at being made the scapegoat of Murrayfield. My answer then, as it still is now, is that I did not like it one little bit, no more than any player would like being singled out from amongst fifteen others who had by no means covered themselves with glory.

However, the Welsh selectors were well within their rights to drop me if they considered I was not worth my place on current form, and indeed I can honestly say that I have never lost any sleep over losing my place in a team; in fact this usually redounds to my advantage in that I make a greater effort to correct what I am doing wrong, and, in addition, play that much harder in an effort to get back in favour. That is another tip I'd hand on to an up-and-coming player - never worry about being dropped; it happens to everyone sooner or later, and if in your case it's 'sooner', then take encouragement from the fact that you can look for and eradicate mistakes in your game before they become fixed habits.

I was not, I'm afraid, quite so philosophic over the other outcome of Murrayfield, which was the widespread belief that I am purely an attacking player who cannot tackle to save his life. Now I've no illusions on the subject of my rating in the rugby game, whether League or Union, neither am I blind to the fact that a good many people will be induced to buy my book mainly in the hope that I will comment on this much-discussed aspect - or, if you like, deficiency - in my play. Obviously I am the last to disappoint cash customers, so here goes. If you don't agree with me when you have heard my side of the story, at least you will have to give me credit for putting all my cards on the table.

First of all, let me say straight away that I've never fancied myself as a Jackie Matthews or Ryk van Schoor in the *tackle*; on the contrary, to me rugby football is essentially an attacking game. In my case this has meant that I have always had two main objectives - staying on my feet, and positioning myself in the most favourable position for essaying the break-through or capitalizing on an opponent's error.. 'Fair enough,' you might reply, 'but you can do your quota in defence as well.' To this I would answer, 'In theory yes, but not always in actual practice.' To illustrate my meaning, let us assume that I'm playing at centre three-quarter in a team that is enjoying an equal share of the ball from the scrums and elsewhere. Theoretically, of course, all I have to do in a case such as this is to lie up close to the scrummage or line-out on our opponent's 'loose head', and lie back for attack on our own 'loose head'. To me, that is an over-simplification of the situation, because I am convinced that attack or defence, as the case may be, is not so much a matter of technique and method as an *attitude of mind*.

In other words, I'm afraid I am inclined to think in terms of attack even when the situation seems to cry out for a concentration on defence.

That, I suppose, is largely why my marking and tackling of an opponent was not always as tight as it might have been. I use the past tense because my experience in the professional game, where there are no winging forwards to cover up deficiencies in midfield defence, has taught me the importance of man-for-man defence in the back line. Players like Jack Matthews, van Schoor, and Rugby League's Doug Greenall can, I grant you, turn defence into offence with a heavy tackle that jolts the ball from an opponent's grasp; a case in point was Ray Cale's tackle of Jack Kyle in the Triple Crown 'decider' in Belfast in 1950, to which I have already referred. Such players, however, are experts at this particular phase of the game, and I, quite frankly, am not.

I can, believe me, tackle effectively enough when I've felt the need pressing, but I prefer to concentrate my endeavours on the scoring of tries rather than their prevention. After all, I don't suppose Stanley Matthews worries over the fact that no one places him in a niche alongside John Charles as a header of a soccer ball. Not that I compare myself with one of the greatest athletes of any game, but it does lend support to the view that 'you can't have it all ways'.

8

BACK IN FAVOUR

A free trip to Paris as reserve for the Welsh team which played France at Colombes, in the last international of the disastrous Welsh season of 1950-1, encouraged me in the belief that I had not blotted by copybook irrevocably with the Welsh Rugby Union.

That of course was good to know, for the coming season was a very special one as the fourth South African Springboks were due to make a tour of the country. Naturally that made me even keener to win back my place in the National XV.

In the meantime, having completed my National Service with the Navy, I had found employment with a motor-coach company at Penarth where the local manager was none other than my tour colleague, Bleddyn Williams. Now Bleddyn I regard as one of the greatest centre three-quarters I have ever had the pleasure of watching and, rugger apart, I count him as a great personal friend and sportsman. Yet I am sure he will forgive me for saying that the only Williams who counted for me in that motor-coach office at Penarth was a Miss Maureen Williams. Maureen was then Bleddyn's secretary - and later became my wife.

Inevitably, perhaps, the fact that I had gone to work at Penarth stated a whole spate of rumours concerning my future as a rugger player; in fact the Press boys had no end of fun with a Newport-Cardiff serial that went on for several weeks. One day I would open my newspaper to read that I was certain to join Newport, and then, the very next day, equally certain to throw my lot in with Cardiff. One writer, in fact, went as far as to declare that he would eat his hat publicly were I not a member of the Cardiff XV within a certain period. If he did so, however, it must have been after I'd departed North for, as everyone knows, I played solely for Llanelly from the time I left the Navy in September 1951 until my departure for Leeds in the November of 1952.

Why my decision to join Llanelly should occasion the surprise and comment it did at the time I find rather difficult to understand. As far as I was concerned the only choice lay between two clubs - Neath, who had given me my first opportunity in first-class rugby, and Llanelly, which was the nearest club to my home at Gorseinon. What influenced the final choice was, I suppose, the fact that my brother Alan was playing for the Llanelly club, but this apart, I happen to hold pretty strong views on this 'hogging of stars' business in amateur rugby.

Every player, I feel, should as far as he is able place his services at the disposal of the first-class club operating in the area in which he lives. Candidly, I never entertained the idea of joining either Cardiff or Newport, and I think it would be a good thing for Welsh rugby as a whole were certain players a little more heedful of their true and natural allegiances.

King of Rugger

You can ignore, too, the stories that I received all manner of 'perks' and emoluments for playing for the Stradey club - they treated me well, of course, but within the letter of the W.R.U. constitution. Certainly the job I obtained as a lorry driver at the Carmarthen Bay Power Station after I had left Penarth had absolutely nothing to do with the Llanelly club.

* * * * *

I was extremely keen to make the Welsh XV against South Africa, and I accordingly put all I knew into the early season matches with Llanelly.

Captained by the Welsh international back-row forward, Ossie Williams, we had a useful if not a world-beating XV, with, in the typical Stradey tradition, a number of clinking good forwards. Even in those days R.H. Williams, then a twenty-one-year-old R.A.F. officer, was revealing more than a hint of form that has subsequently made him one of the kingpins of the Rugby Union game, whilst in Ossie Williams, Peter Stone, and Peter Evans we had an all-international back row - and a fine one too.

The really outstanding performer in the Llanelly pack in those days, however, was the young Ammanford University student Roy Williams, who must have been a certainty for the Welsh front row had he not elected to turn professional. Roy joined Wigan and I still cannot understand how it came about that he was allowed to drift out of the Rugby League game, for he seemed to have everything it takes to make an international prop-forward. The Llanelly backs, though not as impressive as our forwards, were useful, and in Raymond Williams we had a potential match-winner. With a fine turn of speed, a swerve, and an uncanny knack of being on the spot when an opponent dropped a pass, he scored some remarkable tries.

On a Tuesday afternoon in October came the biggest match of the season, or in fact of any season, the meeting with Basil Kenyon's fourth Springboks, the first South African side to visit Wales in twenty years. It was intriguing to recall that the last South African side to play at Stradey - Ben Osler's third Springboks - had done so in 1931, the year that I was born. My rugby-loving father could little have imagined as he watched that team in action that I should be playing against their successors.

At Stradey, however, on the mild afternoon of October 23rd, 1951, I was less concerned with the past than the present, and there was plenty to be concerned about, for it ever a rugby team looked the part it was these large, bronzed, and green-jerseyed South Africans. Whatever the appearance or quality of the opposition, however, there is always a confidence at Stradey that the 'Scarlet' will rise to the occasion, and so they did this time. Unfortunately, we soon found that it required far more than the typical 'Sospan' verve and *élan* to rattle, much less defeat, these rugby-playing robots from the veldt.

In fact, I would say that the fourth Springboks were the best-drilled and most thoroughly disciplined team I ever played against. I have of course faced many teams which have possessed infinitely more colourful individual players, and I have also played with and against teams which could give the South Africans several pointers on attacking back-play, but never have I encountered a team which played the game with such calculating efficiency.

It was obvious from the start that every individual had been well grounded in the game's basic principles, that everyone of them was prepared to eschew heroics in the interests of accuracy, and that the team as a whole possessed a most exact appreciation of what they could reasonably expect to achieve, or not achieve, on a rugby field. For sheer power and tactical efficiency their pack was the finest I've seen in any class of football, and it was out in force against us at Stradey that afternoon. Against Koch, Kenyon, Muller, du Rand, Delport, and van Wyk, our own forwards, bravely and energetically as they played, really had no hope. Their opponents were not only top-class forwards individually, but collectively became a huge battering-ram scientifically wielded and directed. Our chaps, I think, did extraordinarily well to hold them to a margin of 20-11, particularly so when taking into account that the underfoot conditions were reasonably firm and dry and so of course to the Springboks' liking.

Apart from the accuracy I've already mentioned, I was rather less impressed with the South African backs, and during the course of the Llanelly match I gained the impression that they could be rather easily spreadeagled by anyone who was prepared to chance his arm on the unorthodox. As things turned out, this was an impression later confirmed during the course of the Welsh match, but unfortunately not until it was too late to have any bearing on the outcome.

There was, as usual on these occasions, something of a furore over the selection of the Welsh XV for this match, which the newspapers were describing as for the 'Rugby Championship of the World', and not for the first time in my career I was one of its 'storm centres'.

To begin with it looked as though I had been 'placed on the shelf', for when the team was originally announced the chosen centres were Bleddyn Williams and Malcolm Thomas with one of the wing positions left open, presumably for the selectors to have an opportunity of watching Swansea's Horace Phillips in action for his club against the Springboks on the Saturday preceding the international. Over the week-end the feeling was that

Horace, on his form that afternoon, had done enough to earn his place, but in the end the selectors picked me.

I would be the last to argue that the choice was a universally popular one. It was, at the best, a compromise, and I think the Welsh selectors were influenced more than anything by the fact that the side contained no recognized goal-kicker to vie with South Africa's famous 'Ockey' Geffin. I was naturally glad to get a place for this most important match, though for obvious reasons I do not relish playing on the wing. I was really sorry for Horace Phillips, who on the season's form was as good a wing three-quarter as any in Wales, a strong and fast runner who would never fail in a bid for the corner for want of trying.

Altogether it was a Welsh XV that banked heavily on known form and experience. Gwilliam, for instance, had been restored to the captaincy, and apart from myself he had in the side eight of the team which had won the Triple Crown in Belfast two years earlier. In fact the only new cap was the Swansea skipper, Len Blythe, at open side wing-forward, and Len only a week earlier had already covered himself with glory, with a rousing display against the Springboks at St Helens.

History records that we lost the South African match at Cardiff Arms Park by six points to three, but that I'm afraid is an understatement, for we didn't so much lose it as simply 'chuck it away'.

For once at least on the tour, those magnificent South African forwards met their match if not their peers, for our forwards, superbly led by Gwilliam, played the game of their lives. In the line-outs Roy John topped everyone, our great front row of Hayward, Dai Davies, and Billy Williams was indestructible; Rhys Stephens was wherever the forward battle was at its most ferocious, whilst Len Blythe and Alan Forward tackled and covered as though they had a £1,000 side-stake on the outcome.

85

King of Rugger

Thanks to our forwards we had enough opportunities to have won the match, yet we failed, the reason being purely and simply a matter of tactics hopelessly misguided. I have always been an intense admirer of Cliff Morgan as a footballer, but I'm afraid I called him a few names under my breath during the course of the South African match. The tactics he used that afternoon were, in my opinion, not only completely foreign to his nature and outlook, but a help rather than a hindrance to the Springboks.

I appreciate of course that Cliff took several bone-crunching tackles from Basie van Wyk during the course of the match, but that does not altogether explain his complete obsession with kicking that afternoon. Worse still, it was mostly badly directed kicking which besides making Johnny Buchler look a world-class full-back (which he was not) absolutely squandered the chances our forwards were winning for us by superhuman endeavour in the scrums, mauls, and line-outs. The irony of it was that when Cliff reverted for one brief moment to type, Bleddyn and Malcolm made a sorry mess of the Springbok defence with a beautifully contrived scissors movement.

It was then too late, for South Africa had gone ahead with a fine try by 'Chum' Ochse, and a well-taken dropped goal by Brewis. The Welsh try to me was ample confirmation of the impression I had formed in the Llanelly match, that the South African defence was always vulnerable against opposition who were prepared to look beyond the horizons of the orthodox. More's the pity that we didn't try the experiment earlier, for thanks to our forwards we were getting enough of the ball to justify the employment of a ruse or two.

From a personal point of view, this was one of the most frustrating matches I ever played in, for I knew then, as indeed I did at Llanelly, that I had the legs of Paul Johnstone, who was playing opposite me. If that savours of the boastful, then let me assure readers that I never underestimate any opponent, but I've played enough rugger of all descriptions to realise that Paul was not quite the super footballer he was sometimes reckoned to be. 'If only I could get a worthwhile pass', I thought over and over again as the game wore on, but then for all of us in the Welsh jersey that afternoon it was a match of 'might have beens', and for that matter always will be.

With our aspirations to a 'world title' baulked, we turned now to the possible consolation of a victory in the Home International Championship, the first hurdle in our way being England at Twickenham. Rightly so, most people thought, the side which had met South Africa was chosen again *en bloc*, which meant of course that I was retained on the wing. At the last moment, however, Bleddyn, who seems to have his own private 'Twickenham Bogey', was forced to withdraw and after some most regrettable and uncalled-for indecision on the part of the Selectors Alun Thomas, the clever and resourceful Cardiff centre, was awarded his first cap.

Poor Alun, how they made him suffer for his honour! The news that Bleddyn had had to withdraw broke on the Friday evening, yet Alun - the official reserve for either centre position - was not told that he was playing until a few minutes before the kick-off, and only then after a hurried selectorial conference held (we are told) in a very *private* corner of the Twickenham grandstand.

In the meantime, all manner of weird and wonderful things had been happening. Jack Matthews had been wired for back in Cardiff, whilst the hapless Thomas, who had not been included in the Saturday morning team talk, did not know whether to eat a light lunch or a heavy one, always assuming that his nerves allowed him to eat at all! A bad show, and an unnerving one for the player, which speaks much for Alun's temperament that he was able to celebrate his first international with such a fine display.

Earlier in this book I have referred to Twickenham as one of my lucky grounds; this time, however, it was anything but, for within minutes of the start, as I accelerated for the ball, I felt an excruciating stab of pain in my thigh, and hobbled off to the touchline where trainer Ray Lewis diagnosed a badly pulled muscle. With a man out of the pack, Wales were finding if hard to contain the England forwards, and even before nerves had steadied themselves on either side England had scored twice. Each time it was the burly Wasp's wing, Ted Woodward, who was the instigator. On both occasions he churned down the Welsh right flank like a Sherman tank, the first time slipping the ball inside to Agar, who scored, and on the second crashing over himself. England were now six points ahead, and the prospect seemed bleak for Wales. In the interim my thigh had been strapped so as to relieve the worst of the pain, and I returned to the field.

No doubt with an apprehensive eye on Woodward, John Gwilliam directed wing-forward Len Blythe to stay with me as a help-mate on the flank. England were still very much the aggressors, and they were in fact scrummaging in our half of the field when Cliff Morgan suddenly demonstrated to everyone present that his form in the South African match had all been a bad dream. Receiving the ball from Rex Willis near our twenty-five, he slipped his man on a threepenny-piece, and veered outwards around the flank of the English centres with a surge of speed that was thrilling to watch. On he went, straightening his course en route, up to and past the half-way line where Ken Jones on his inside took a short pass and galloped forty yards with Agar in futile pursuit. Malcolm converted from in front of the posts, and Wales were back in the game with a real chance.

With the England side still reeling under the impact of this unexpected blow, Gwilliam revealed one more example of his shrewdness as a leader. At this critical moment he ordered Len Blythe back into the pack for a full-out offensive, and once again the forwards responded with the same fighting spirit they had shown against South Africa. They were great, those Welsh forwards, and in my mind's eye I can still see Rhys Stephens and Don Hayward descending on poor Gordon Rimmer as he picked up the ball in mid-field - they reminded me of a pair of hungry lions disputing the sharing of a victim.

England, however, were giving nothing away, and it looked as though the tremendous efforts of our pack were once again to count for nothing. Then it happened!

A scrum went down near the touchline on my side of the field, just outside the England twenty-five; Willis passed swiftly, and I came in as fast as I was able to try and make the overlap. It could be that the England mid-field defence were surprised by my rather unexpected intervention, but whatever the reason, they hesitated that vital split second, and the ball travelled swiftly and accurately along the Welsh line to Ken Jones, who fairly flashed by the startled full-back Hook to score in the corner. Once again Wales had pulled it off at Twickenham, and if there were special heroes then they were the whole Welsh pack, Ken Jones, and Cliff Morgan..

I had to miss the Scottish match at Cardiff, but Alun Thomas, a most versatile player, made a more than adequate deputy, and some fine place-kicking by Malcolm Thomas (eight points out of eleven) enabled Wales to win fairly comfortably, and establish, of course, another stake in the Triple Crown and Championship for the season. As in 1950, the 'decider' was once again in Ireland, though on this occasion at Landsdowne Road, Dublin.

King of Rugger

For one reason or another, it was not a very confident Welsh party that made the sea crossing to Ireland. To begin with, two of the key players in our previous wins were out of the reckoning through injuries sustained in the Scottish match, Rex Willis having broken his jaw, and Len Blythe with a knee injury. Rex was replaced by a new cap, the tough Monmouthshire Valleys player W.A. Williams, then playing for Newport, whilst Len's place was filled by his club mate Clem Thomas, who had received one cap as a teenager against France a couple of seasons previously.

Quite a burden rested on the shoulders of Clem Thomas, for it was his job to look after Jackie Kyle, never an easy task. There were also misgivings over the composition of the three-quarter line, for with my thigh injury healed the selectors had brought me back to the wing position. This meant that Alun Thomas was moved back to his rightful position at centre to the exclusion of Bleddyn Williams, who had occupied the position in the Scottish match. Needless to say this caused a rare old furore, and altogether there seemed little of the customary optimism.

In the true Hibernian tradition Ireland started off fast and furious, and it was evident that popular Desmond O'Brien was bent on making a first-class show of what promised to be his last international as his country's captain.

Possibly his boys were too anxious to give him the right type of send-off, for they were quickly penalized for an infringement on the touchline. My kick, thank goodness, was bang on the mark; three points for Wales, and our tails were up. When the whistle went for half-time we were nine points to the good, for first Clem Thomas had hared away from a line-out to put Rhys Stephens over, and then Cliff Morgan and Ken Jones had worked a perfect replica of their masterly effort at Twickenham.

The doubters were being confounded at all points, for

Alun Thomas was piling into Noel Henderson like a slimmer edition of Jack Matthews, Clem Thomas had Jack Kyle in his pocket, whist the new man, Williams, was serving Cliff Morgan with splendid length and accuracy.

In many ways Landsdowne Road, 1952, was an anti-climax because Ireland were not the force they had been two years earlier, and it was no surprise when near the end Roy John romped over their goal-line for a try which I converted. Fourteen points to three was the final margin, which meant that eight of us, John Gwilliam, Ken Jones, Malcolm Thomas, Roy John, Don Hayward, Dai Davies, Gerwyn Williams, and myself, all of whom had taken part in the thrilling match at Belfast two years earlier, had had the wonderful satisfaction of being members of two Crown-winning teams.

As in 1950, the stage was now set for a grand Championship finale with the French, only this time at St Helens, Swansea.

Once again we were blessed with a lovely spring day, perfect in fact for rugby. More's the pity, therefore, that what the large, expectant crowd actually witnessed was a thoroughly inept and disjointed exhibition from the Welsh team. Indeed I shall always regret that my last appearance in the Welsh jersey coincided with one of my bad days, when I missed my tackles, my passes, and even my goal kicks. True, we won in the end, but only on the strength of a drop goal by Alun Thomas, and two penalty goals belatedly kicked by myself. Against this, France scored a try which was converted. In the first half, while they still retained the services of their very clever scrum half Gerard Dufau (he fractured a collar bone), they were obviously the better side.

So ended my international career for Wales in Rugby Union. I had enjoyed every minute of it - yes, even my one bad and only visit to ill-starred Murrayfield!

9

THE BIG CHASE

During the weeks that followed my first appearance for Wales at Twickenham, my father began to develop the trace of a North Country accent, or so it seemed! Certainly he might easily have done so, for hardly a week passed between January 1950 and November 1952 without him having to answer the door to someone connected with the professional game.

Although I seldom had any personal contact with the various agents who used to call at my home so frequently, I was particularly impressed with the persistence, and indeed with the methods, of a certain gentleman who shall be nameless.

Regularly once a week he used to write me letters stating that this club or that were interested in me, never however making any concrete offer - that, presumably, would have come had I agreed to negotiate. The thing that struck me as odd, though, was the form of the correspondence! Writing in a numbered duplicate book, the gentleman concerned would retain the original draft and send me on the flimsy copy. This strange procedure conjured up, for me at any rate, the picture of a harassed agent, surrounded by mountains of duplicate books, searching frantically for his last letter to a player in whom some club was interested.

In the beginning, of course, neither I nor my family were even remotely interested in a professional career. To begin with Mum and Dad considered, rightly at the time I'm sure, that I'd received a good enough education to get by in the world without the necessity of making a rugby career. I had obtained my School Certificate at Gowerton, and if that wasn't the peak of academic achievement it was at least, so we thought, a fair enough foundation upon which to seek a decently paid job.

After my success in my first season of Big Rugby we were, too, to a certain extent, misled by the wonderful promises that were made concerning jobs and prospects in South Wales. When I embarked on my National Service, I did so in the hope, if not the expectation, of being found a decent job on my release. As I say, there had been promises. I knew, too, that no first-class Welsh club is without its influential personages, who, I reasoned, would fix me up satisfactorily wherever I decided to play my rugby.

The more fanatical apostles of amateurism (who incidentally are seldom found amongst the ranks of those who have actually played the game) will of course instantly remind me that the laws of Rugby Union distinctly prohibit anyone obtaining a job on the strength of his ability at rugby football. This is indeed the case, but you cannot legislate against human nature, which is precisely why a rugby-minded employer will always go that little bit out of his way to find a job for a 'star'. It did not, however, work out that way for me. Not that I'm grumbling; on the contrary, I am merely stating the main reason which influenced my final decision to turn professional.

When I came out of the Navy the best job I could find at first was with a motor company, where the prospects were to say the least remote. This was followed by a lorry driver's job at the Carmarthen Bay Power Station which, even though it had the virtue of being free and easy, was not the best of bets, either for the present or the future.

Another factor which originally made me rather wary of offers from the Rugby League was the highly lurid accounts of the conduct of the professional game which I had gained, second-hand I'll admit, from various sources. From these I had formed my own impression of the League code, an impression which would rightly have very much angered my Northern friends had they known me at the time. I pictured it as a game for thugs administered by thugs, a game in which £ s. d. was the first, the last, and the only consideration. A game in fact in which violence and sharp practice existed in exactly equal proportions.

This was of course a hopelessly inaccurate picture, which was first corrected for me at, of all places, the celebrated 'Long Room' of the Lord's Cricket Ground.

I was playing at Lord's for the Navy against the Army in the July of 1951, and in the course of a group conversation in the Long Room at the close of play was introduced to a well-spoken and quite charming Yorkshireman whose enthusiasm for games was self-evident from the moment I started talking to him. His name was Kenneth Dalby, and amongst other things he was the team manager of the famous Leeds Rugby League club. Not that we discussed the possibility of my turning professional on that occasion; on the contrary rugby football was, as I remember it, only a small part of our conversation.

At that moment I little dreamt that Mr Dalby was going

to play such an important role in my subsequent career, but nevertheless my meeting with him had most certainly corrected many of my erroneous beliefs on the subject of Rugby League football. I remember thinking at the time that if Ken Dalby was a typical example of a League official, then it could not be the thugs' game some people would have one believe. Happily the years were to prove me right, for few persons in any walk of life have extended me the same friendship, kindliness, and understanding that my family and I have invariably received from this very fine Yorkshire gentleman who so ably presides over the destinies of the greatest club of them all, Leeds.

There were, however, to be many eventful happenings, a number of them humourous, before I eventually made the plunge.

I remember when I was at Devonport receiving a summons to appear before the Commanding Officer, Captain R.W.. Marshall. With my conscience not always as clear as it might have been, I was not entirely without misgivings when I presented myself to the old man. He was brief and to the point. 'Look here, Jones, (and my heart sank), 'I've had a couple of fellows here looking for you. They say they're from a Rugby League club!' (I sighed with relief; none of my sins had been discovered anyhow). The old man went on, 'Yes, they were from the Rugby League, so I had them escorted out, and turfed overboard.' He waited, presumably for me to digest the full enormity of the fate that had overtaken two strangers on my special account, and then went on, 'For you own good, you know, my boy; all right, you may go now.'

Captain Marshall in his own gruff way was, I'm sure, acting with my best interests at heart, just as my Dad did when he actually ejected a particularly offensive person from our home at Gorseinon. Let me make it plain though that neither my father nor any other member of our family resented the legitimate enquiries of the accredited representative of the clubs interested in me. What my family did object to, and strongly, were the frequent intrusions on their privacy by touts who were obviously playing one club against another in an effort to make a bit for themselves. Believe me, there are plenty of these characters in the game, and it is they who bring the Rugby League into disrepute in South Wales, not the club directors who, in my experience at least, are in every instance the soul of honour, courtesy, and discretion..

It was in November 1952 that the hunt for my services really intensified, and what with one thing and another I was becoming increasingly more inclined to talk business. Rugby football apart, I could not see myself making any kind of a niche for myself in South Wales; then, too, I hoped to get married soon, and this above all gave me an incentive to do the best I could for myself.

For days the Leeds club, through their intermediary W.J.Jones, the former Llanelly and Oldham star, had been endeavouring to obtain my signature, with the result that our sitting-room at Lime Street often resembled a conference-room. Needless to say, this was a worrying and unsettled period, and looking back on it now I realize what a wealth of gratitude I owe my father who all along thought of nothing but my own interests. He was a tower of strength during the most important and eventful days of my young life. The fact that my brother Alun was captaining Llanelly didn't make matters any easier, and if that seems a small consideration beside several thousand pounds, I can only say that we Joneses of Gorseinon were a typically Welsh family, and proud of it. This meant that we were not blind to the honour, and the loyalties it demanded, of captaining a club with as great and long a tradition as Llanelly's.

My father, brothers, and I talked the matter over far into not one night, but many, and finally intimated to W.J. that I was ready to discuss terms with the directors of the Leeds club. That did it! W.J. telephoned Leeds, Mr Dalby and the club secretary Mr Hirst there and then chartered a hire care and hastened to Gorseinon, which thereupon became the Mecca for every Press man in Wales, and indeed of one or two from outside the Principality.

For hours we sat and discussed the pros and cons of the matter in our sitting-room, until the final decision was made and I agreed to join Leeds in exchange for a lump sum. The amount? Well I'm afraid I can't disclose that, even six years after the event, for the contract I have with the club still has a year or two to run, and one of its original conditions was that I did not disclose the exact terms. Sufficient to say that the newspapers were correct in describing it as a record, and that I have never at any time since had any reason to feel dissatisfied with my end of the bargain.

The scenes in Gorseinon that night were, they tell me, something quite out of the ordinary, and I am also told that the licensed houses did quite a roaring trade as the football fraternity gathered for the 'inquest'. Meanwhile, vastly relieved that it was all over, I was on the way to Penarth with one contract in my pocket, and with the means to another - an engagement ring.

10

THE NORTH NOT SO GOLDEN

On Friday morning, November 7th, 1952, having broken my journey from Gorseinon to share the momentous news with Maureen, I boarded the train for Leeds, and a new career.

With me for company went my brother Cliff, and the warmth and numbers of the reception committee that greeted us at Leeds station on that raw November evening was quite literally overwhelming. Everyone was kindness itself, the club had fixed us up at the quite sumptuous Queens Hotel, where in foyer, cafeteria, and stairway I was repeatedly buttonholed by perfect strangers who shook my hand and wished me a successful career in Rugby League.

I was tremendously impressed by the spontaneity of it all, although it made me wonder whether I could possibly live up to what was obviously expected of me. Except for the Rugby League Instruction Manual through which I'd browsed on the train journey to Yorkshire, I had little idea of the conduct of the thirteen-a-side game, and knew even less of its tactics and subtleties. Obviously I was anxious to gain my first experience of it as quickly as possible, and although Mr Dalby and Secretary Mr Hirst had decided that I should assimilate the 'atmosphere' by sitting in the stand for Leeds' match with Keighley, they readily agreed to my request that I should play.

Incidentally, friends back in Wales frequently ask me how my new colleagues reacted to the presence amongst them of a 'glamour boy' with an exorbitant price tag on his head. All I can answer is that, while I cannot possibly vouch for the Leeds players' private feelings, they treated me from the start as one of themselves, and one and all did everything possible to help me settle down in my new environment. Arthur Clues, the skipper, in particular was perfectly marvellous, but I will be writing more about this aspect of professional rugby later.

I played at full-back in the Keighley match, and found it a very queer experience to field a ball near my own goal-line, yet not be able to bang it straight down into touch. What helped me here was the length of my punt, for although kicking duels between full-backs in the League had long since gone out of fashion, I quickly tumbled to the fact that if I could drive the ball far enough upfield to make the opposing full-back turn around for it, I was at least keeping out of trouble. Not very subtle stuff, of course, but it saved me making a fool of myself! Then as the game progressed, and Leeds began to assert their undoubted supremacy, I was encouraged to have a run or two upfield to link up with my own backs.

By and large, I was not really displeased with my debut in Rugby League. I suffered under no delusion, though, that the professional game was going to be a 'picnic', for even my brief taste of it had convinced me that it was going to call for a far higher standard of physical fitness than I'd required as an amateur.

King of Rugger

That was not my only discovery for in my next couple of matches I found, amongst other things, that the marking and tackling were generally speaking much keener and more brusquely applied than in Rugby Union, that opponents caught on very quickly to your methods and favourite ruses, and that professional rugby was far more scientific than the amateur game.

I was very lucky in the sense that I was allowed to do my learning gradually in a successful side, and moreover in a side whose members spared no effort to make my indoctrination as painless as possible. I am indeed grateful to Arthur Clues and the rest of the team for their patience and understanding in my early days as a professional. As a result I seemed to be settling in satisfactorily, even if I wasn't setting Headingley alight, when along came calamity in the shape of an injury that was to set me back a very long way indeed; indeed I sometimes thought to the point of No Return.

The accident happened on the Batley ground at Mount Pleasant where I had pulled a leg muscle only a few Saturdays previously. This time, however, there was far worse in store for me - a compound fracture of the forearm which put me in Leeds Infirmary for the next few weeks, and out of football for the rest of the winter. As is so often the case with a really severe injury, it happened in the simplest way imaginable. I was struck off-balance in a tackle, falling awkwardly with the ball lying across my forearm. I had fallen in an identical way scores of times in the past, but on this occasion, I suppose, the distribution of weight and the angle of my fall were just that little bit different. So there it was, my first major injury at rugby, and altogether a pretty pickle for a club which had but recently paid a record-breaking fee for my services.

This latter aspect of the business worried me

considerably during the summer months I spent convalescing, for although I had all along felt confident of eventually making the grade in professional football, I wondered if this injury was going to retard the process. And if so, would the Headingley club and its following have the patience to wait. Possibly I got too keyed up over the whole business, or perhaps I had a subconscious fear that the arm would go again in the first heavy tackle I sustained. Whatever the reason, my return to the Leeds side at the start of the 1953-4 season was a complete flop.

I began as a centre three-quarter but could do nothing right. I dropped my passes, missed my tackles, whilst whenever I spotted a gap in mid-field it seemed miraculously sealed at the split second I essayed my break. It was, I suppose, the timeworn case of nothing going right for the player out of form. Team Manager Ken Dalby and his directors must, I feel sure, have felt a qualm or two as they watched me blunder my way about the Headingley arena. Whatever their private feeling, however, to me at least they never betrayed, either by word or gesture, any anxiety that I would turn out one of the biggest failures in Rugby League history. On the contrary they endeavoured to restore my confidence by playing me at full-back. The move was unsuccessful, however, for even here I was completely out of touch, so much so that there was finally no alternative but to relegate me to the 'A' team.

In retrospect I feel that this was my 'darkest hour' in rugby football, for not only did I feel that I had let down the Leeds club, but in addition the many people back at home whom I knew were following my career in the North. To be perfectly honest, I also knew that there were several people back in Wales who would look upon my failure as a professional as a personal vindication of their own views on Lewis Jones the footballer, so with one thing and another my omission from the Leeds team worried me a lot more than did my omission from the Welsh XV after Murrayfield. Every cloud, however, has its silver lining, and though I might have doubted this at the time, the proverb applied, to some extent at least, in my case.

Understandably, perhaps, I had blamed my poor form for Leeds in the opening matches of the 1953-4 season on the injury sustained at Batley back in the previous January.

I was, I suppose, partially justified in doing so, but as it turned out the injury, or more accurately the lay-off from football it enforced, was to have a beneficial effect on my career in the Rugby League. From January until May I was able to sit in the stand or on the trainer's bench and study at my leisure, as it were, the whole technical set-up of thirteen-a-side rugby. I'll grant that on my return to the game this study did not seem to have brought any worthwhile results, but I am convinced that in the long run it was of inestimable value to me.

Indeed I would go as far as to recommend that every Rugby Union player who transfers to the League should be granted, as far as humanly possible, an acclimatization period such as the one I was able to obtain through injury. Atmosphere is this particular context is, I consider, as important as technique, for once you have been absorbed and become acclimatized to the Rugby League atmosphere you immediately start taking a live interest in its tactics and techniques.

11

THE WAY BACK

Leeds are a great club. That much is, I think, accepted throughout the world of Rugby League football, and if I were asked to enumerate the reasons for their greatness, I would begin by pointing to the wonderful loyalty and team spirit that permeates the whole Headingley organization, from 'star' to the last recruit to the club nursery.

Thus even when a player has been relegated to the reserve team, he is still made to feel an important and accordingly valuable, member of the organization as a whole. This feeling helped me tremendously in my fight back to the top.

Other important factors of course were the advice and constant encouragement of Team Manager Ken Dalby, and the co-operation of my team mates in the 'A' XIII. Consequently, as the weeks went by, I found myself recapturing much of my old form and confidence, so that at a certain Thursday evening training session I found my name posted once again on the first team list hung up in the dressing-room. This was in early November, almost a year to the day of my turning professional, and the match chosen for my 'come-back' was by any standards a tough one. Warrington, our prospective opponents, who were going great guns near the top of the League table, were tough nuts to crack on their own vast concreted stadium at Wilderspool.

It would, of course, round the story off in the best fairy-tale tradition were I able to write that I was the hero of a really sensational victory at Wilderspool, but in professional rugby, at least, things seldom happen like that. The most I can say is that as a team we made Warrington go all the way for their narrow victory, and that I kicked three goals and scored a try, as part of the Leeds' contribution. Far more important to me, however, than the points tally was my all-round form at centre three-quarter. My reflexes seemed to have sharpened considerably since my last appearance in the first team, with the result that I was once again seeing the gaps and spurting through them with no thought of failure.

The Leeds team as a whole were, during the Warrington match, gearing up to the tremendous form in which they totalled well over 300 points in ten matches. Indeed the Saturday after the game at Warrington we ran riot to the tune of fifty-six points against Hull Kingston Rovers at Headingley; then on to Belle Vue where we defeated Wakefield Trinity 46-5, and finally back again to Headingley where we crushed Castleford 48-14. 150 points in three matches was terrific football by any standards, and a wonderful come-back for me as my personal tally in the three matches stood at sixty points, the eye-catching performance being my twenty-three points (ten goals and a try) against the Rovers from Hull.

The lads were really in top gear now, and they took some holding, for it was a team effort in every sense of the word.

In the pack Arthur Clues, Bernard Poole, Bill Hopper, and Willy Blan were well nigh unstoppable, Jeff Stevenson was playing some terrific stuff at scrum half, whilst Gordon Brown, who had displaced the Headingley idol Dick Williams at off-half, was a strong rugged player capable of forcing those half-openings on which centres thrive. With me in the centre was another rugged and reliable customer, the Australian Keith McLellan, and then on the wings were strong go-ahead players like Ted Verrenkamp (another Australian), George Broughton, and Drew Turnbull.

For sheer poetry of motion I don't think I have seen a wing three-quarter quite like Drew, who joined Leeds as a comparative unknown from the Scottish border club, Hawick. He gained top honours in Rugby League, and in the process scored something like 250 tries for the club at an average of nearly one a match. Drew was as fast and determined as most on his forays down the Headingley touchline, but what to my mind distinguished him from the rest was that spectacular and often hair-raising dive for the corner when he'd reached striking distance. Drew, airborne, was a spectacle that brought the house down at Headingley, as indeed on every ground he played on. The tragedy of it was that the very intrepidity of his methods made him prone to injury, and in the end his confidence suffered accordingly. But for injury, I'm quite certain that Drew Turnbull would have been one of the major successes of the Australian trip in 1954; as it was, however, he was forced to return home in advance of the rest of the party.

Certainly the 'Blue and Ambers' of Headingley had struck one of their purple patches, for apart from a rather unlucky set-back in a hard-fought match at Thrum Hall, we went from early November until Christmas undefeated, while the rugby we produced was, it was agreed on all hands, really vintage stuff.

Christmas was a really bumper one, for in the three

holiday matches with Huddersfield, Wakefield, and Batley we ran up 102 points, of which my own share was fifty-one, mostly from goal kicks. The Christmas Day game with Batley at Headingley I particularly remember because I felt the Mount Pleasant team owed me something, not only for the leg injury I had sustained in the corresponding match exactly a year previously, but also for the compound fracture I had received against them a month later. Drew Turnbull was evidently of the same mind, for after a week or two of indifferent form he came back into the side to outstrip the Batley defence for six glorious tries, whilst I got another, and kicked seven goals to help in a 44-5 win for Leeds. Honour was satisfied with a vengeance.

By now I was beginning to think that all my troubles in Rugby League football were now behind me, and to make my cup of personal happiness really full, there came the news of my first honour as a professional - the invitation to play for Wales against France at Marseilles on Sunday, December 13th, 1953. The Welsh XIII that afternoon was:

Glyn Moses (St. Helens), Arthur Daniels (Halifax), Les Williams (Hunslet), Lewis Jones (Leeds), Malcolm Davies (Leigh), Ray Price (Warrington), Billy Banks (Huddersfield), Captain, John Thorley (Halifax), Tommy Harris (Hull), Eynon Hawkins (Rochdale), George Parsons (St. Helens), Bernard McNally (Rochdale), Glanville James (Hunslet).

It was interesting to reflect that out of the thirteen supposedly top-notch Welshmen in the Rugby League at the time, only Les Williams, George Parson and myself had worn the Welsh international jersey as Rugby Union players. It was, as I say, interesting, if only as a reflection of the wisdom and astuteness of the League's talent spotters who in most cases had induced the players North before they had played sufficient first-class football to attract the Welsh selectors in the Union game.

Since the majority of the Welsh team at Marseilles originated from the outlying Monmouthshire and Llynfi Valleys in Wales, I could not help wondering whether the Welsh Rugby Union Selectors pay as much attention to the players of the unfashionable clubs in these areas as they do the players of the big clubs in the thickly populated industrial areas. Certainly it seems that many a Valley player has attracted the attention of professional scouts a long way in advance of the attentions of his own Selectors. At Marseilles on the afternoon of my first international Wales were slightly unfortunate, for although we scored four grand tries through Arthur Daniels (two), Malcolm Davies, and Ray Price, with goal kicks from me to bring the points tally up to twenty-two, France with their great speed and opportunism kept well in the hunt. With only seconds to go they finally snatched victory with a try by their flying winger Contrastin, 22-23 and hard luck, Wales.

Back again to Yorkshire and the North, where on the strength of our brilliant and consistent form, many people were tipping us as likely winners of the Rugby League Challenge Cup at Wembley. Everyone at Headingley would have given much for the honour, if only for the sake of our grand Australian skipper, Arthur Clues, who was desperately anxious to round off his wonderful career in England by being the player to lead Leeds to the honours that had eluded the famous club for so long.

We started off our quest with a home tie against - yes, you've guessed it - Batley, and perhaps due to over-confidence received the shock of our lives, for the Mount Pleasant boys, playing well above the form they had revealed against us over the Christmas holidays, fairly romped home to a 20-13 victory. Fortunately for us the 'two-leg' system gave us an opportunity to make amends, and there was a capacity house at Mount Pleasant to see us attempt it. With pep talks from Ken Dalby and Arthur Clues still tingling in our ears we got down to business from the word go, and in three minutes were ahead with a try by Ted Verrenkamp after fellow Australian Keith McLellan had forced the gap in mid-field. Our tails were well and truly up now, and Batley, surprised no doubt to find such totally different opposition from the lacklustre side they had encountered only a week earlier, simply had no answer to the power play of our pack, abetted by backs who were constantly switching the direction of attack. Although Batley lost the services of their centre three-quarter, Frain, who was sent of following an altercation with the referee after a tackle on Drew Turnbull, I doubt whether even at full strength they could have held Leeds on our form that afternoon. In the end we won 23-6, so that we had turned our seven points deficit into a winning margin of ten points.

Leigh were next on the agenda, and a tremendous battle it proved to be on the mud heap Headingley was that afternoon. Our forwards, though 'Clueless' through injury, were magnificent, Bill Hopper in particular playing what I rate as his greatest game for Leeds. A point down at half-time, and held for most of the second half by Leigh's tremendous tackling, we finally broke clear to score two tries, giving Leeds a win, 12-3. Captain for the day in place of Arthur Clues was Gordon Brown, and appropriately enough it was he who first broke through the vice-like grip of the Leigh mid-field tackling.

Once again the draw was kind to us, and this time it was Workington Town, captained by the immortal Gus Risman, who came to Headingley. On this occasion too the lads produced a power display, 'power' being the operative word where Arthur Clues was concerned, for I can see him now crashing over the Workington line draped with three opponents almost as big as himself. Jeff Stevenson too had a great match at scrum half, streaking downfield time and again as only 'Stevo' can streak. For all Gus's craft, and the strong running of Gibson and Tony Paskins in the centre for Workington, it was clearly Leeds' day, and the margin 31-11 brooked no dispute over our right to enter the semi-final.

This chapter, which I've entitled 'The Way Back', began with an encounter with Warrington. There unfortunately it also has to end, for at Wigan in the semi-final the 'Wires', with Ray Price and the great Australian wing Brian Bevan at their scintillating best, were once again too good for us. It was perhaps some consolation for us that Warrington went on to win the Challenge Cup in the course of a replay with Halifax at Odsal Stadium. Even though I would dearly loved to have crowned my 'come-back' with an appearance at Wembley, the man I was most sorry for, as was every man jack at Headingley, was lion-hearted 'Digger' Clues, who had once again been pipped almost at the post.

12

AUSTRALIA-BOUND ONCE MORE

During a rugby football career which has brought me into contact with (often far nearer than I would wish) some of the world's greatest players, I have only encountered one who tackled with quite the same shattering and deterring impact as my former Welsh International Union colleague Jack Matthews.

This was the St. Helens 'king-pin' Douglas Greenall, and he oddly enough, as much as any single person, helped ensure me my ticket for Australia with the 1954 British Rugby League party. Except possibly for Wooloongabba, all the best things in life seem to happen to me at Headingley, and my encounter with Douggie in the First Tour Trial, February 1954, was not the least of them.

Thanks in great measure to a well-timed service from my Leeds club mate, Gordon Brown, who was playing at off-half for the 'Reds', I was given a yard or two to move in, which of course is always a desirable thing when you are faced with a tackler of Douggie's lethal character. As a result, I suppose I did well enough against Doug to convince the tour Selectors that I could survive in face of Australian tackling.

To compensate for Leeds' failure in the Challenge Cup Final, and to set the seal on my 'come-back' as a player, I thus had the honour of becoming a Rugby League 'Lion', the final composition of the party being announced as follows:

Full-backs: E. Cahill (Rochdale Hornets), J. Cunliffe (Wigan).
Wings: W. J. Boston (Wigan), A. Turnbull (Leeds), F. Castle (Barrow), T. O'Grady (Oldham).
Centres: D. Greenall (St. Helens), P. Jackson (Barrow), E. Ashcroft (Wigan - vice-captain), B. L. Jones (Leeds).
Stand-off halves: R. Price (Warrington), R. Williams (Hunslet - captain).
Scrum-halves: A. Burnell (Hunslet), G. Helme (Warrington).
Prop forwards: J. Henderson (Workington), A. Prescott (St. Helens), J. Bowden (Huddersfield), J. Wilkinson (Halifax).
Hookers: T. Harris (Hull), T. McKinney (Salford).
Second-row forwards: B. Briggs (Huddersfield), G. Gunney (Hunslet), C. Pawsey (Leigh), N. Silcock (Wigan).
Loose forwards: K. Traill (Bradford Northern), D. D. Valentine (Huddersfield).

The critics agreed that there had been no major surprises, for although Billy Boston had only played something like half a dozen matches in the League since he had left South Wales to join Wigan, his class had become obvious to all in the course of the Tour Trials. In some quarters surprise was expressed at the inclusion of Dickie Williams, who had been awarded the captaincy. His form early in the season had cost him his place in Leeds' side, and there was a feeling that he was perhaps 'over the hill'. However, it was generally agreed that Dickie (now at Hunslet), still a fine player, had developed into a shrewd 'general', and no doubt this had a direct bearing on his selection. As for myself? Well, I reckoned I had earned my ticket, if only for remaining hale and hearty after my meeting with Doug Greenall at Headingley.

Led by two highly experienced administrators, Messrs. Hector Rawson (Hunslet) and Tom Hesketh (Wigan), our party left London Airport by B.O.A.C. air liner on the Thursday evening of May 13th. This was the first time in history that a British Rugby League team had made the journey by air. After a twelve-hour delay caused through our inability to land at Rome, our scheduled first stop, owing to fog over the airport there, we landed at the Mascot Airfield in Sydney with mere hours intervening before the first game of the tour with a Western Districts XIII at Bathhurst on Wednesday, May 19th.

As we expected, the match was no more than a 'pipe-opener', and we won comfortably 29-11. Even so, there was clearly trouble in the offing for, as the penalty awards (twenty-six to our opponents, and six to ourselves) indicated, referee Doug Cohen was far from satisfied with our interpretation of the rules - particularly the 'play the ball' rule.

Neither was the game entirely free from incident, and one burly Lions' forward was continually in the wars both with the home players and their voluble and very partisan supporters. On this occasion, and subsequently, the Australian Press went to considerable pains to enlarge on the incidents; however, taking the broad view, this is perhaps a common aspect of Press-touring team relations in almost every country, for a touring team is inevitably the cynosure of all eyes, and the players' conduct both on and off the field accordingly becomes News with a capital N. If the Australian Press are a little more lurid in their treatment of such incidents than most, it is perhaps because they lean towards the American headline type of presentation on most topics. As for the differences in rule interpretations, that too is, I suppose, inevitable, and the onus is surely on the visitors to conform, as far as they are able at least, to the customs of their hosts.

The second match of the tour was one which we regarded with a great deal of foreboding, and with good reason too, for our opponents, the tough Steelmen of Newcastle, had victories to their credit over both the 1936 and 1946 Lions and, as it turned out, over the 1954 Lions as well. Our fellows, obviously badly rattled by the tough tactics of the local forwards, and rather more by some rather odd refereeing decisions, went down by twelve points to ten. Only a narrow margin, it is true, but nevertheless Newcastle were full value for their win, and spirits drooped amongst the Tourists accordingly.

On the credit side, however, was a fine confident display from Ernie Ashcroft in the centre, and some brilliant running from Frank Castle and Drew Turnbull on the wings. Drew unfortunately was to pull a thigh muscle badly in the very next match against Riverina at the sheep-country town of Wagga Wagga, an injury which was to render him inactive for the whole of the tour. This was bad luck indeed for a winger whom Australian crowds would undoubtedly have admired intensely, for if there is any feature of his rugby the Aussie really relishes, it is the spectacle of a class wing three-quarter going full bat for the corner flag - but then don't we all? Riverina were beaten rather more easily than the score of 36-26 might at first suggest, for with Ernie Ashcroft again in superb form, our backs ran in for eight tries whereas Riverina's scores came mainly from the highly practised boot of former 'Kangaroo' Test winger Johnny Graves, who kicked seven goals.

King of Rugger

I had not played at either Newcastle or Wagga, but was brought in as a wing three-quarter for the match with Sydney representative XIII on the Sydney Cricket Ground, and thus for the first time on the present tour was brought face to face once again with the typical Big Match atmosphere in Australia.

As in 1950, my impression was that the real Lions were on the paying side of the pickets, and I did not envy the experience of the several chaps in our side who were facing it for the first time. There were, according to official sources, 50,889 people in the Sydney Cricket Ground that afternoon, and from the volume of noise and the nature of the comments hurled over the pickets it would seem that all but the odd 89 were rooting solidly for the Sydney boys. The home team responded valiantly and were well worthy of their eventual victory by 32-25.

It was a fine tussle, and a happy return for me personally to this world-famous sporting arena, for I scored a try and kicked five goals. Even so I could not match Test full-back Clive Churchill who landed seven, and fully justified his reputation as one of the greatest of full-backs.

From Sydney to Wollongong where we were held to a draw by the Southern Districts team in a match distinguished by two brilliant tries scored by the young Oldham winger Terry O'Grady. On each occasion Terry careered half the length of the field beating man after man with a bewildering body swerve. From Wollongong we returned to Sydney where a week before the First Test on the Sydney Cricket Ground we were defeated 11-22 by a New South Wales representative team which included eight of the men who were to play against us in the Test match.

Needless to say, with three defeats in our first six matches, the 1954 British Lions did not lack for critics. Obviously we were not happy with our own displays, and in an effort to tighten things up for the forthcoming Test matches our managers invited former Kangaroo centre three-quarter Ross McKinnon to take charge of the coaching arrangements, a move which caused a lifting of eyebrows in certain quarters, though the move was certainly not without precedent. South Africa's Danie Craven, for instance, coached the Rugby Union Wallabies during their tour of the Veldt country in 1949, and there are, I believe, any number of examples of touring teams deriving tactical assistance from people in the country they happened to be visiting. Sufficient to say that Ross McKinnon placed his valuable time, and great enthusiasm, unreservedly at our disposal, and I'm sure that most of us benefited from his advice, particularly where the interpretation of certain of the laws were concerned.

Form and coaching, however, were far from being the only problems that bothered our Selectors on the eve of the First Test match, for our casualty list had been mounting ever since the tour started. With Turnbull, Cahill, Greenall, Dickie Williams, and Tommy Harris all on the injured list it was rapidly becoming a question of who to include rather than of whom to omit. Finally all the arguments, selection problems and what have you were resolved, and the British team which lined up in front of the green-and-gold-jerseyed Australians and 70,000 wildly excited spectators on the Sydney Cricket Ground was: Cunliffe, Jones, Jackson, Ashcroft (captain), Castle, Price, Helme, Prescott, Mckinney, Wilkinson, Silcock, Valentine and Traill.

The Australians immediately set a cracking pace, and almost before we had adjusted ourselves to the feel of things they were ahead with a try scored by a second-row forward, after scrum-half Holman and the young prop-forward Duncan Hall, playing in his first international, had combined splendidly. Soon, however, we turned the tables with a fine break by Davy Valentine who passed to Nat Silcock for the burly second ranker to blast a way over near the posts. I converted. From then on the match developed into a terrific struggle, with the crowd roaring their heads off as thrill followed thrill and play swept from end to end.

Australia were next to score, when Bull, an aptly named prop-forward, charged through the ruck to send O'Shea over near enough the posts for a try, which Noel Pidding converted without undue effort. Pidding shortly afterwards made it 10-5 for Australia with another fine kick from a penalty awarded forty yards out, and that was the position when the bell went for half-time. With a breeze in their favour the lads attacked strongly from the restart, and we were rewarded with a beautifully worked try by the Old Warrington firm of Gerry Helme and Ray Price who exploited some bad positioning by one of the Australian centres to make the man over - in this case Barrow's Phil Jackson. once again I converted, and we were level at 10-10, but only briefly for ace kicker Noel Pidding regained the lead almost immediately with a truly magnificent penalty goal kicked into a fairly strong breeze from a distance of fifty yards. I promptly replied with a similar effort from the same distance, though of course with the wind, and the stage seemed set for one of the great Test Battles of post-war history. What actually developed, however, was rank anti-climax! Our defence, which only minutes before had looked so compact and resolute, cracked wide open, and sweeping through came a tidal wave of green and gold. In the brief space of ten minutes we were quite literally overwhelmed, for in that time Hall, Pidding, and McCaffery (twice) had all crossed our line, and each time the deadly Pidding kicked the goal.

The score was now 32-12, and the position irretrievable as far as the Lions were concerned; yet just to make sure, up came Clive Churchill to join his three-quarters in a movement that put winger Carlson clear once again of the field, for Pidding to convert. It had been a great day for Australia, and an even greater one for Noel Pidding whose personal contribution of nineteen points (eight goals and a try) represented a world record for Rugby League Test football. The irony of it was that Noel might easily have drifted out of football earlier in the season when his club, St George, decided to dispense with his services. At the conclusion of the First Test most of us, I think, were uncharitable enough to wish that he had been allowed to do so.

Inevitably, there was a large-scale 'inquest' in the Australian Press, who as usual were not over-fastidious in their choice of adjectives. Here is an example. 'In a few words England was walloped in every department of the game. It would require a treatise on English literature with a copious use of superlatives to describe the nature and quality of their play. It did not get out of the kindergarten stage. It looked like the effort of 'J' grade players in a suburban church competition playing for certificate of merit at the annual Christmas break up in the curate's vestry. I am now satisfied that this English team would not reach Test standard - no, even if the Archangel Gabriel was standing over them with a flaming sword exhorting them to the crack of doom.'

Good strong meaty stuff, and we liked it, even though we could scarcely be expected to agree. Indeed we considered that we'd already confounded quite a few of our critics by holding our much-fancied opponents for something like three parts of a game fought at a cracking pace. We considered, too, that we were at last running into something approaching our English form, a view endorsed in print by that grand Australian centre Trevor Allen, who had enough experience of our game back in England to know what he was talking about. Our point of view was just about summed up by our skipper-for-the-day, Ernie Ashcroft, who in a Press interview said, 'To us the scores merely represented Australia's dominance over the last twenty minutes or so, but there are two more Tests to go before the Ashes are decided.'

Meanwhile, as far as the Lions were concerned, the great hero of Sydney had been the Huddersfield loose forward Davy Valentine, who had endeared himself to a crowd even as hard-bitten and partisan as Sydney's for his indestructible spirit, and non-stop covering and tackling. Indeed the thought occurs that if we had had half a dozen Valentines at Sydney, the scores would have been reversed and more. The plain facts were, however, that we didn't, but there it was - and even in defeat there was hope for the future.

13

RETURN TO WOOLOONGABBA

The first match in a scheduled eight-match itinerary of Queensland was a floodlit encounter with a Brisbane XIII, and with Gerry Helme, Terry O'Grady, and Billy Boston touching peak form we ran up thirty-four points against the locals, who could only show a couple of goals in reply.

This was, needless to say, a victory that put us in good heart for the important State match with the full Queensland representative team five days later. Whether it was the beautiful sunshine, or whether the boys had been nettled by their critics back in Sydney it is difficult to say, but the certain thing was that the team hit top form from the moment we arrived in the State. Queensland were reputed to possess their strongest team in years, but we were far superior than the actual margin of 34-32 in our favour might suggest. This in fact was our most convincing performance to date. The 27,000 Queenslanders, a record for Queensland outside Test matches, simply revelled in our brilliant back play.

King of Rugger

Gerry Helme and Dickie Williams combined splendidly at half-back, Phil Jackson was in top form in the centre, whilst Billy Boston, who scored three fine tries, was a particular favourite with the crowd. As at Sydney, however, it was Davy Valentine who really brought the house down with his rugged all-action performance at loose forward, and his try, a brilliant piece of work in which he slipped five opponents, was most generously applauded, as it deserved to be. For me, too, the game had been something of a personal triumph, for my bag of thirteen points (five goals and a try) was only three short of the Rugby Union world record I had established on this same 'Gabba' ground four years earlier.

On the Sunday following the State match the boys, without me this time, ran riot to defeat Wide Bay 60-14, Terry O'Grady running in for five tries, and Billy Boston for four, whilst in addition Jack Cunliffe kicked nine goals. In high good humour and confidence we travelled North where our first opponents were the Southern Zone XIII at Mackay - a seaport town of some 12,000 inhabitants, looking out on the Great Barrier Reef.

It was not, however, as a geography student that I remember Mackay, but rather for goings on that were distinctly Wild Western in character and setting. To start with there was the game, played against rugged opponents and before an audience even more so; we won that all right by 28-7, my own tally being five goals, and two tries from the full-back position. It was a match more distinguished, I'm afraid, for violence than for the quality of the football, and following a series of incidents which did no credit to either side, one of the players was ordered off. Altogether it was not the most pleasant of football matches, but one, we later discovered, which was not altogether out of character in the neighbourhood it was played in.

As soon as the game was over, and we had changed and eaten, we were invited to sample a little of the local hospitality.

In no time at all we found ourselves bang in the middle of the kind of scenery they used to depict in the old silent westerns. The saloon we found ourselves in had, in fact, the identical swing doors the villain used to kick open with the cry of 'reach', and the characters who thronged the bar were, to say the least, hardly the type of chaps you would invite to tea on a Sunday afternoon back home in Wales. Unshaven for the most part, they tossed off whacking great schooners of beer at a single gulp, whilst their conversation was more in the vein of Ernest Hemingway than Godfrey Winn.

Perhaps they weren't really bad fellows at heart, but then we never had time to find out. As we stood around chatting in a group, a particularly rugged-looking character, who had obviously drunk rather more than even he could consume, approached the two Lions forwards, Jackie Henderson of Workington and his buddy Jack Wilkinson of Halifax, and made a couple of highly lurid as well as uncomplimentary remarks on rather intimate topics. Just as Henderson prepared to remonstrate with him the character broke his glass on the bar in the approved 'free-for-all' style, and took a swipe at Jackie, who sustained a nasty-looking if not serious gash on the ear. This obviously was too much for Jack Wilkinson, who put on a Victor McLaglen act of his own - and a highly effective one too - for the drunken Digger was *hors de combat* before he could raise his glass for a second swipe. No one seemed to turn a hair while the fracas was in progress, and things were right as rain afterwards. But I for one would, I'm afraid, find the night life of MacKay rather too hectic for my taste.

From 'brawling' let's get back to rugby, and a Sunday fixture at Townsville against a North Queensland XIII. This match was noteworthy for the return to form of skipper Dickie Williams, who until then had been nothing like the mercurial genius of his great days at Headingley. The backs, too, were as a unit slipping really into Test gear, Boston and O'Grady getting four tries apiece and Phil Jackson one.

My tally was six goals, though with the Second Test only a week away I was not completely satisfied with my goal-kicking. One match in fact remained before the Test - a mid-week encounter with Central Queensland at Rockhampton under floodlights. 'Encounter', perhaps was the word best fitted to another rough and violent match which often erupted in fisticuffs, and worse. We won without a great deal of difficulty, but as a Test match run-out it was a failure. Worse still, it cost the Lions the services of two valuable players, Jack Cunliffe and Ted Cahill, both of whom sustained injuries. Even so, the most regrettable accident in a regrettable match was the injury sustained by the Queensland player Tynan, who damaged a vertebra during a fracas on our goal-line towards the end of the match.

Yet despite the fact that the rugby sometimes got a little out of hand, we enjoyed our stay with the hospitable Queenslanders, and at Townsville especially we were seldom stuck for entertainment or diversion in our off-duty hours.

Fishing was one of the big attractions, and the title of ace angler was claimed by Doug Greenall who, along with Jack Wilkinson, Brian Briggs, and Charlie Pawsey, used to spend hours at his favourite pastime, though certain carping critics used to allege that all four used bait that was much bigger than any of the fish they caught. Though dreadfully unlucky with injuries St Helens' Doug was proving himself the ideal tourist, and he and Terry O'Grady were in great demand as soloists at concert parties. There was one thing, however, that Doug would not do, and that was go bathing. Having listened to the tale of the local swimmer who had had a leg bitten off by a shark, Doug decided there and then that he was not running that risk - 'I have never seen a one-legged centre three-quarter, and I don't fancy being the first,' was his way of putting it.

Before we had returned to our H.Q. at Brisbane for the vital Test, Australia had announced their team which, except for the substitution of Hazzard for the injured McCaffery at centre, was the same as the one which had won at Sydney.

As usual on this tour, our own choice was made relatively simple by injures - Boston and O'Grady for instance were the only two wingers available, myself the only fit full-back, and Tom McKinney the only hooker. In fact it is highly likely that the only decision that caused the Selectors any heartburning was the decision to bring back Dickie Williams to the off-half position in place of his fellow Welshman, Ray Price, who had played a particularly brilliant game at Rockhampton just before the team was chosen. They might also have had a qualm or two over the omission of the young Hunslet forward Geoff Gunney, who was running into first-class form at the time. But by and large the Australian Press seemed to accept the chosen XIII as the best available, though in most cases they gave it but slim hopes of beating Australia at the 'Gabba'.

Australia in fact stood a great chance of making a bit of Test history by clinching the series with two straight wins, and in the expectation like as not of seeing them do it thousands of New South Walians had made the long journey to Brisbane, inevitably a city very much in the throes of the Big Match fever. The morning of the match saw the weather change from sunshine to drizzling rain, but that didn't dampen the ardour of the ticket speculators as they plied a brisk trade in Black Market tickets outside the stadium. As usual, too, the well-wishers thronged the foyer of our hotel on the morning of the match, amongst them Ray Lindwall with his young Lancashire-born son Raymond, and Bob McMaster, the former Wallaby prop who had been one of my team mates at Headingley.

Rain was still falling as Keith Holman kicked off for Australia, and straightaway Ernie Ashcroft took us into the attack with a cracking burst up the middle. Churchill nailed him in the twenty-five, and as the ball went loose Noel Pidding crashed into Dick Williams before the ball had even reached him - a penalty to us, and I couldn't miss from straight in front of the posts. In rapid succession Boston, Jackson, and finally Pawsey were all hauled down inches from the Australian goal-line. At this stage we were right on top, but as is so often the case it was our opponents who actually scored, Carlson racing out of his twenty-five, punting over my head, and retrieving before either I or Boston could recover our balance on the wet turf. Pidding as usual converted, and against the run of play we were three points to the bad. Not for long, though, for receiving a pass on the blind side of a scrum in his own twenty-five, Oldham's Terry O'Grady baffled half a dozen Australians with a beautiful body swerve and hared forty yards downfield up to Churchill before passing to Charlie Pawsey, who hurled himself over. The kick was from the touchline, but this was Wooloongabba and the ball flew straight between the posts. 7-5 to Britain - the lead was ours, and as things turned out we never lost it.

Five minutes later we were on the move again, a brilliant run by Davy Valentine, followed by a neat scissors between Phil Jackson and Billy Boston, enabling the latter to side-step Churchill and run thirty-five yards to the posts. Once again my kick was true, and although Australia hit back with a try by Provan, converted by Pidding, we were still retaining a solid grip on the play and retaliated with another penalty kicked by myself and a splendidly worked try by Dickie Williams which I again converted.

Half-time came with the score 19-10 in our favour, and already the Kangaroos were coming in for a little barracking from their disappointed followers which seemed to goad them to extra effort, with the result that the opening minutes of the second session found us pinned down in our own quarter.

After some fairly hectic exchanges near the goal-line, prop forward Duncan Hall fastened on a loose ball and hurled himself over. It was now the Lions' turn to be incited and the outcome was a beautifully contrived try from Billy Boston after Dick Williams and Ernie Ashcroft had worked a dummy standing pass in mid-field. Again the angle was acute, but once more the special gremlin of Wooloongabba was at my side to guide my kick unerringly between the posts.

A moment later he surpassed all previous efforts on my behalf, for after Dick Williams had run elusively in mid-field and found me with a long pass, I feinted to the touchline, swivelled round, and plonked over one the sweetest drop goals it has ever been my pleasure to kick on any rugby field. We were unstoppable now, and straightaway Ernie Ashcroft careered half the length of the field to send Phil Jackson in for me to kick my eighth goal, and then almost from the kick-off I got my ninth - another Wooloongabba 'special' - a drop goal from almost the identical spot as my first one.

The Lions were properly rampant at this stage, and the final twist to the Kangaroos' tail came in the shape of one of Gerry Helme's lightning breaks from the scrum and a try under the posts. The goal formality, as it was, was my tenth and enabled me to top the previous individual scoring record in Tests between Britain and Australia - strange that I should have achieved this and a similar record in Rugby Union Test football on the same Wooloongabba ground in Brisbane. I can't help wondering whether there is at this very moment on some deserted Welsh village football ground some unknown youngster practising goal-kicking as I used to do as a schoolboy back in Gorseinon, and if so, will he too, in the fullness of time, go on to play for Britain at Wooloongabba, and in the process leave my records far behind? It is an intriguing thought, and for Wales's sake I hope it comes true.

Back for the moment, however, to the seething excitement

of Brisbane on Saturday, July 3rd, 1954. Enthusiasm mounted as a badly beaten Australia pulled themselves off the floor for the last desperate rally. First Holman, then Carlson, breached our not now so vigilant defence, and Pidding kicked a goal. It was a gallant resistance but still only a token one and when the bell came the giant scoreboard showed Great Britain 38, Australia 21 - sweet retribution indeed for the indignities of Sydney less than a month earlier.

The critics who only a short while before had been belabouring us as 'the worst Touring team ever to leave England' were, to do them justice, equally ready to pay tribute to the brilliant play of the Lions at Brisbane, and amongst those whom they deservedly singled out for special mention were Gerry Helme, nowadays at his brilliant best at scrum half, Dickie Williams (also in the Second Test far more like the player of his heyday), Phil Jackson and Ernie Ashcroft, who had outplayed their opposite numbers, and Leigh's Charlie Pawsey, who had been quite literally a 'lion' in the tough forward battles.

With one apiece, and one to play, a sell-out was assured for the decider at Sydney in a fortnight's time. Meanwhile one of the three matches that confronted us before the Final Test was in effect a Test in itself. The meeting was with the New South Wales State team which had already defeated us earlier in the tour and which is, of course, in any year you like to mention, virtually representative of the full strength of Australian Rugby League.

Inevitably the game aroused tremendous interest, and a crowd of real Test match proportions greeted the Lions at the Sydney Cricket Ground. The atmosphere was so electric that, though I was one of those being 'rested' for the Test proper the following Saturday, I could almost feel the pangs of 'Big Match nerves' as I sat with the rest of our 'casualty department' and watched our boys line up amid the bedlam around them.

From the very start the keenness of the 'spotting' and the brusqueness of the tackling made it obvious that the 'needle' was really in between the two teams, but no one I think was prepared for what actually happened - a stand-up fight between the two teams which caused the match to be abandoned with over half the time left for play. I've seen some spectacles on a rugby field, but never one quite like this where the players simply stood in mid-field squaring up to their opposite numbers. It was quite fantastic, and the referee, maligned as he was at the time, had, I'm afraid, no option but to call it a day.

Neither did the affair finish at that, for long after the teams had bathed and changed the crowd milled around the dressing-rooms and Ray Price, who had been subjected to considerable abuse by a faction of the crowd during what play had taken place, was actually man-handled as he left the changing-rooms, an incident which had his team-mate and bosom chum Billy Boston really fighting mad. Indeed, after sorting out at least a couple of Price's assailants, Billy had to be forcibly restrained from getting to grips with the remainder.

It was all very regrettable, and while I am not disposed to apportion the blame on one side more than another, I do feel that the Australian Big Match atmosphere, which is far tenser and partisan than our own, does impose a considerable strain on the players - a strain, in fact, that is often insupportable for the young player. I suppose that it also had some significance that our opponents were in line to earn something like £30 a man for a win against us, whereas our own remuneration was by the tour rules only a third of that. However, reasons and degrees of culpability apart, events on the Sydney Cricket Ground that afternoon did nothing to suggest that the vital Final Test on the same ground, due to be played seven days later, was going to be a 'picnic' for anybody.

14

ASHES FOR AUSTRALIA - AND NEW ZEALAND FOR US

Darcy Lawler of Sydney was as able and impartial an official as I ever saw in either Rugby League or Rugby Union, yet nothing will ever turn me from the conviction that it was a couple of errors on his part that lost us the Ashes on the Saturday afternoon of July17th, 1954.

The first of them occurred during the first half hour of the game when, with a lead of eight clear points and our confidence accordingly mounting, we were robbed of a certain three points, possibly five, by one of the most blatant pieces of obstructionism I've ever encountered on a rugby field.

After Ernie Ashcroft had broken clean through the middle and kicked over the head of the advancing Churchill, the Australian defence had been cracked wide open, the mere formality of Terry O'Grady reaching the ball and touching it down was all that was needed for a try. To our amazement, however, Terry, as he came racing in, was picked up bodily, without the ball, by a giant Australian

A Lewis Jones 'special' - and it's two points for Great Britain, but it's a
Test match and a vital one, hence the expression of anxiety on the face
of his team-mate, Jack Grundy

N.B. All photo captions are as per original book

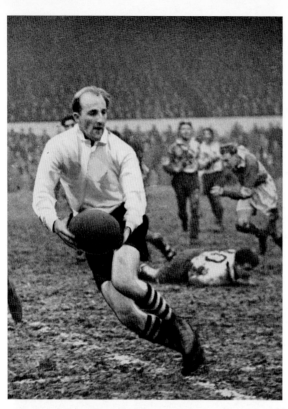

Left: One of the most important stages in the author's career. In this picture, Lewis Jones is seen making one of the baffling runs that were a feature of the final Australian Tour Trial in 1954.

It was his magnificent display in this match that induced the Rugby League selectors to take him on what proved (for the author) a record-breaking tour of Australia and New Zealand

The author, with Quinn running up in support, being chased by Boston, the Wigan winger, in the Rugby League game between Leeds and Wigan in October 1957

Even Test rugby has its social side - the author relaxes over a drink with his two Australian Tour colleagues, Tom Harris (Hull), *centre*, and Alan Davies (Oldham)

Not the Grand National - merely the Leeds players' method of showing their elation at setting foot on the classic turf of Wembley. They were just as elated a few hours later when they defeated Barrow in the final of the Challenge Cup competition.

A gathering of the stars - and the clans. The author with *(left to right)* Richard Murdoch, Donald Peers, and Brian McLenaughan during the Rugby League tour of Australia

Five Headingley V.I.P.s. Cup Final day is approaching and five of Headingley's key men break off a tactical talk to pose for a picture. *Left to right:* the author, full-back Pat Quinn, second-row forward Don Robinson, team manager Ken Dalby, and skipper Keith McLellan

Leeds (in striped jerseys) file out alongside their opponents Barrow for the 1957 Cup Final at Wembley. The author is [fourth] in the line [led by] his captain Keith McLellan

British Rugby
League Touring
Team, World
Cup series,
Australia, 1957.
Back row:
P.T. Harris,
M.J. Sullivan,
A. Davies,
G. Moses,
A. Rhodes,
R. Price.
Middle row:
D. Turner,
S. Little,
J. Grundy,
G. Gunney,
E. Ashton,
J. Whiteley,
W.J. Boston.
Front row:
T. McKinney,
P. Jackson,
W. Fallowfield
(Manager),
A.J. Prescott
(Captain),
H.E. Rawson
(Manager),
J. Stevenson,
the author

FOUR PHASES IN GOAL KICKING

Above: Placing the ball

Below: The approach

Above: Correct position for kick

Below: Well away

Left: A family group - the author with his Welsh wife Maureen and young son Kevin

Below: Lewis Jones the second? Father wonders as he occupies (for him) the unfamiliar role of placer

second ranker and to our even greater amazement Referee Lawler ruled 'penalty' when the deliberate nature of the offence simply cried out for the award of a penalty try. As it happened I was wide with my kick so we got nothing from a movement that had try written all over it from the moment Ashcroft's kick bounced behind Churchill.

That was error No. 1, and error No. 2 came at a similarly vital moment, early in the second half, when, with Australia leading 10-8, we were battling hard to turn the tables. Harry Wells, who had been playing a strong thrusting game in the Australian centre, burst through inside our twenty-five, but was firmly nailed inches outside our goal-line by a double tackle effected by Valentine and Bowden from behind. Down he came like a ton of bricks, with the ball still grasped to his side - a lucky let off for us, I thought, yet Harry (and you can hardly blame him, after all) had different ideas and after at least three separate efforts he finally succeeded in inching the ball onwards to the chalk line. All this, of course, happened far more swiftly than it takes to tell, and I am accordingly prepared to believe that the referee gave a 'spot' decision which he genuinely believed to be correct at *the moment he arrived at the scene* (the italics are mine).

Back in my own South Wales old men never tire of recounting the story of the try that was disallowed New Zealand in the historic match with Wales at Cardiff Arms Park in 1905, and it is related that Deans the New Zealand centre continued to claim, even on his death bed, that he had actually scored. I mention that because I feel just as convinced, and I will still be fifty years from now, that Harry Wells did *not* score a legitimate try against us on the Sydney Cricket Ground on July 17th, 1954.

I do not claim that we deserved to win this particular Test match for there were, I'll grant, deficiencies in our play that afternoon - my own goal-kicking, to mention but one of them

- but I do feel that we easily might have done so had these vital decisions gone our way. Still, as Don Bradman said of umpires, 'It's *always* the losing side who criticize the quality of the umpiring.' Sufficient to say that we had gone down fighting hard, and with the score at 20-16 the Aussies must assuredly have been as thankful to hear the final bell as we were downcast. It had been a good, hard, and, happily in view of previous happenings on the same ground, clean and sporting encounter, and as we congratulated Clive Churchill when it was all over we really meant what we said.

Certainly those Australians, under the guidance of coach Vic Hey, had shown themselves a superlatively fit lot, and it was easy to see the tremendous influence of the former Leeds star at work in the performances of our opponents' centres, Harry Wells and Alec Watson, who both took a great deal more holding than we were sometimes able to manage. I also thought Keith Holman at scrum half very good, but I will not subscribe to the opinion of a large section of the Australian Press that he was the 'World's Greatest in that position' - that indeed was a bold statement to make during a series that also contained the quick, elusive genius of Gerry Helme. As a unit the Australian forwards had, generally speaking, been faster and more together than our own, but individually none of them surpassed Dave Valentine and, perhaps to a lesser degree, Alan Prescott, who had both got through a tremendous amount of work in a most gruelling match. There it was, then, no Ashes for Britain but a by no means ignominious failure.

A mere three days after the tumult and excitement of the Final Test match at Sydney the Lions were across the Tasman Sea in New Zealand, where we met an Auckland Maori XIII at Whangarei in the first game of a ten-match itinerary, and thanks mainly to the fine work of Ernie Ashcroft were seldom extended to win 14-4 in very heavy going. Only three days later we were lining up before the full New Zealand representative side for the First Test match before over 30,000 fans at the Carlaw Stadium, Auckland.

Again the going was very heavy, which added if anything to the superb merit of Billy Boston's finest Test performance - four fine tries - and how he skimmed over the mud to get them! Terry O'Grady, too, had a splendid match, repeatedly flummoxing the New Zealanders' defenders with his body swerve and intrusions into the line from scrums and play balls. It was also a memorable occasion for young Geoff Gunney, who earned his first Test cap, whilst Tommy Harris, fit again, not only won the scrums but bounded all over the field with the irrepressible energy the fans back home know so well. The final score was 27-7, a truly first-rate performance, for the New Zealand side, as events were soon to prove, were no one's chopping block.

From Auckland (for the second time in my career) we made the 300-mile journey down to Wellington, at the tip of the North Island, where we simply overwhelmed the Provincial side with fast-running and precision passing. As at Auckland, our wingers, Boston and O'Grady, were in dazzling form with three and four tries apiece respectively as a just reward for their spectacular efforts. Doug Greenall also had a fine match, and his strong running not only brought him three tries but showed that he had fully shaken off the effects of the nasty injuries sustained in Australia. The final score was 61-18, and my own contribution eleven goals.

The Second Test match was played at Greymouth on the West Coast of South Island. What a big change from the great stadiums of Sydney and Brisbane! Indeed, one end of the ground was not fenced at all, with the result that the spectators were actually sitting on the dead ball line, and on one occasion a small boy ambled on to the in-goal area when play was actually in progress. Still, spectator amenities have nothing to do with football playing and ours, to be sure, wasn't very good that afternoon, for a New Zealand team which showed five changes from the one defeated at Auckland played a hard bustling game which jolted us unceremoniously out of our customary stride and in the end ran out worthy winners by 20-14, thereby leaving the rubber wide open. I could not help thinking that the New Zealand Rugby League forwards seemed to possess much of the ruthlessness of outlook and method of their Rugby Union counterparts whom I had played against four years earlier.

In Atkinson, Butterfield, and Nulcare the Rugby League outfit possessed a very tough and formidable trio indeed. Even so, my outstanding memory of the Second Test match at Greymouth concerns our first try scored by Terry O'Grady. It was really a 'beaut', as our Australian friends would say. Gerry Helme started it from the brink of our own goal-line with a dummy and a quicksilver dash from the scrum, Doug Greenall developed it with a strong incisive break downfield before passing to O'Grady who shook off his opposite number, Edwards, to finish off a movement that had gone the whole length of the ground.

An easy victory over the South Island representative team at Dunedin came as some consolation for the Test defeat, after which we travelled to Christchurch where we again scored freely to defeat the Canterbury Province representatives 60-14, a match notable for the record-breaking achievement of Billy Boston whose four tries brought his total for the tour up to thirty-six - one in excess of the previous record set by Tom Danby of Salford in 1950. Another feature was the brilliant form at scrum half of 'Ginger' Burnell, and once again the swift elusive running of O'Grady on the opposite wing to Boston delighted the crowd. Twelve tries scored inevitably gave me plenty of goal-kicking practice and eleven 'bulls' out of twelve, plus a penalty goal, reassured me that the old right book was in sound working order for the vital Test. Meanwhile there still remained a couple of matches in North Island, against North Island and South Auckland, and both of them, as it happened, were won by margins ample enough to raise our hopes for the all-important clash with New Zealand at the Carlaw Park, Auckland.

In accordance with the pattern that had frequently shown itself at Greymouth, the Third and final Test proved a tough, rugged, and sometimes over-robust battle, fought for the most part between two fiery packs on a surface churned into a quagmire by heavy rain. Rain fell heavily throughout but it failed to damp the ardour of our forwards among whom Ken Traill and Charlie Pawsey seemed positively to revel in both the conditions and the circumstances. Ernie Ashcroft and Phil Jackson, too, both had fine games in the centre, and in the end the margin of twelve points to six by no means flattered us. Terry O'Grady and Ray Price got tries, whilst I kicked three goals for the Lions against the three penalties kicked by the New Zealand full-back, White.

One game now remained in New Zealand - that with Auckland - and this unfortunately turned out quite the roughest of the lot. At times the whole thing degenerated into something perilously akin to the tap brawl we'd seen in far and remote Mackay in North Queensland, and during its fierce and violent course Nat Silcock and Jack Wilkinson were ordered off. Frankly I failed to see that their misdemeanours were any the worse or more obvious than those of the other ten forwards on view. In the end Auckland were the winners by five points to four and we could not argue other than that they deserved it, for most of the game injury had deprived them of the services of their very capable full-back, White.

From New Zealand it was back again to Australia and the Sydney Cricket Ground where we resumed (by hasty arrangement) our argument with the New South Wales representative team, and although this time at least the game did go the full distance, it was yet nothing to write home about from the viewpoints of gentlemanly conduct and sportsmanship. The fact that the conditions underfoot were again deplorable did not, I dare say, help matters in this respect, for they dictated of course that the forwards should battle things out at close quarters, and with the 'needle' in a certain amount of rough stuff was almost inevitable. At one stage we were leading 12-11, but an injury to Billy Boston, which necessitated him leaving the field for good, put paid to our hopes of revenging the four defeats we had now sustained on the Sydney ground, and in the end New South Wales were worthy and not too hard-pressed winners by thirty-five points to fifteen.

Only two matches now remained, one against the New South Wales Country Districts at Canberra, which we won by 66-21, and a final match at ill-starred Newcastle which, according to custom, we lost 22-28. Again according to custom, it was a rough, tough, and altogether regrettable affair.

As I remarked earlier on it is not my intention even to try to apportion the blame in such matters for after all it takes two parties to produce a 'rough-house' on a rugger field. It could be said that the main guilt rests with the aggressor, but then two blacks do not make a white and in any case it is my opinion that a top-class footballer - or sportsman in any sphere - should possess sufficient self-control to shrug off all but the more blatant fouls and rough stuff. The incidents in Australia, and to a slightly lesser degree in New Zealand, sprang, in my estimation anyway, from a combination of circumstances inseparable from a major tour of this description. The opponents of professional rugby will no doubt make capital of them as an illustration of 'what filthy lucre does to sport', but then - except for the Springbok tour of Britain in 1951 - I cannot think of one major rugby tour that has been entirely free from incident. This is inevitable, I suppose, for in the glare of modern publicity methods the prestige aspect of international competition is magnified out of all proportion to the result.

After-dinner speakers do, I know, still go on maintaining that the game's the thing, and so indeed would most of us like it to be. But if you think that an international team is judged purely and simply on its approach to the game, then read your newspapers on the morning afterwards and reflect on the volume of highly critical abuse that descends on the team unfortunate enough to lose. It will, I think, convince you that success is the main criterion by which a team is judged.

So much then for this unhappy conclusion to a tour which had been in so many of its other aspects thoroughly enjoyable. There may at times have been fisticuffs on the field, and barracking on the side-lines, but I certainly enjoy my rugby in Australia. Their players are tough, fast, and skillful, and I especially love the fearless and forthright attitude to life that characterizes your typical Australian. You know exactly where you are. There are no intrigues or subtleties, a spade is termed just that, and above all they accept you as they find you without research into your background. Yes, I like Australia, and in the same sense New Zealand, and certainly in the rugby football sense both countries have been extraordinarily kind to me.

I'm sure readers will forgive me if I end this account of the 1954 tour on a strictly personal note. In the last two matches I kicked twenty goals (fifteen at Canberra and five at Newcastle), and was thereby able to return an aggregate of 278 points for the whole tour, made up of eight tries and 127 goals. This figure was forty more than the French full-back Puig-Albert achieved in 1951, and fifty-five more than our own maestro Jim Sullivan had established twenty years earlier. Needless to say I was both honoured and delighted to have my name bracketed with two of the greatest of all time.

15

KEEPING ALONG THE ROAD

Although a rather cosmopolitan Leeds XIII led by Vic Hey had defeated Halifax in a wartime final at Odsal Stadium in June 1942 the club, despite many near and heartbreaking misses, had not won the Rugby League Challenge Cup since 1936, when Jim Brough's immortals had triumphed over Warrington at Wembley.

Needless to relate a repeat performance had been the Headingley goal throughout the intervening years, and bitter was the disappointment when in 1947 the side under Ike Owen fought their way through to Wembley only to be defeated 4-8 by Bradford Northern.

Cup fever gripped the city anew in the January of 1957 when it was learnt that we had drawn Wigan out of the hat in the first round of the competition. Fortune favoured us in that the match was scheduled for Headingley and a sell-out was assured as Wigan, who had reeled off twelve consecutive victories, were like ourselves going really great guns in the league. The scenes outside the Headingley turnstiles on the afternoon of the match were reminiscent of those at Cardiff Arms Park on an international occasion and the atmosphere both on an around the arena was electric to match as we lined up as follows:

Leeds: Dunn; Hodgkinson, McLellan, Jones, Quinn; Lendill, Stevenson; Anderson, Prior, Hopper, Poole, Robinson, Street. *Wigan*: Platt; Boston, Ashton, Ashcroft, O'Grady; Bolton, Thomas; Barton, Mather, McTigue, Cherrington, Bretherton, Collier.

Straight away it was evident, if only from the brusqueness of the tackling, that this was going to be real cup-tie stuff with no holds barred. As the packs crashed into each other in their introductory engagements, the impact was actually audible to us in the backs. It looked as though there was going to be a stalemate in the vital mid-field exchanges, too, for while Ashcroft and Ashton could make little headway down the middle they saw to it that Keith McLellan and myself had no chance either.

As is so often the case with these 'needle' games, however, a score came as a result of a solitary mistake after a period of safe and circumspect play. Wigan, as it happened, were the unfortunates in this instance. Following some wary sparring - in order presumably to probe the quality of our defences - they decided to open up from a play-the-ball near the half-way mark. A pass went astray, I was there to kick on, and (memories of Gorseinon Thistle), dribble forty yards to score near the posts. I converted and we were five points ahead - not for long, though, for Wigan retaliated by working the ball out to Billy Boston on the right who just streaked for the corner, by-passing Bernard Poole and full-back Dunn as though they were a pair of wax figures out of Madame Tussaud's.

King of Rugger

It was a tremendous effort and the Headingley crowd, always generous in such matters, thundered their applause so that the earth seemed to quake. Ashton missed the fairly easy kick and, heartened by the fact that we still retained the lead, we swarmed back to the attack. Jeff Stevenson produced one of his snake-like steal-aways from the scrum's base, Jack Lendill and Keith McLellan rocketed a way up the middle, and Pat Quinn contributed a couple of thrusting forays up the left touchline. Altogether Wigan were being pretty hard-pressed to hold us for the remainder of the first half. Then, as their stand-off half Bolton was helped off with a leg injury near half-time, we sensed that the Wigan defence, frequently hard-pushed, was now ready to crack, and so it seemed as our forwards bull-dozed a way to within fifteen yards of the line. Once again, however, we reckoned without the speed and power of Boston, who, receiving the ball on the very brink of his own goal-line, simply tore down the touchline to outstrip friend and foe alike for a truly wonderful try in the corner. Billy must have covered fully ninety yards *en route* and, taking into account the back-to-the-wall circumstances in which it was scored, his try will rank with the greatest I've seen on any rugger ground - League or Union.

Thus Wigan had fought their way back to a one-point lead at half-time, and as the sides lined up for the second half Headingley was one huge seething cauldron of tension and excitement, with spectators spilling over the touchlines in their eagerness to get as near as possible to the tremendous battle that see-sawed to and fro.

At the start things went our way and Pat Quinn was nearly in the Wigan twenty-five. Pat put the whole of his thirteen stone plus behind his thrust for the flag, but Billy Boston - inspired surely that afternoon - fairly hurtled him into touch with a wonderful flying tackle. We were not to be denied, however, and as the ball went loose outside the Wigan twenty-five I picked up, and slammed over a drop goal - 7-6 to Leeds, and the place in an uproar. Still we hammered away at the stricken Wigan defence and a battering-ram burst by Bernard Poole followed by a beautifully timed wide pass to Delmos Hodgkinson sent the young winger racing over for the try that clinched, or so we thought, the issue.

But we quickly learnt afresh that there are no such things as 'certainties' in rugby football. The depleted Wigan team, far from being dismayed by their four-point deficit, threw caution absolutely to the winds and launched a series of non-stop attacks on our goal-line. Even as an opponent I could not but feel the utmost admiration for a side which, though reduced to twelve men, so disdained defence they they even dispensed with a full-back, Platt, the occupant of the position, coming up quite openly into the attacking formation. Wigan's very boldness deserved success, and they got it when Ashton intercepted and forced his way over for Platt to convert - 11-10 to Wigan, and the tension becoming unbearable.

Having regained the lead by adventurous methods, Wigan now (mistakenly, I thought) reverted to the circumspect and orthodox, and after we had forced them back into their own half of the field, Keith McLellan shot through a gap in the centre. Turning inwards to confound the covering defence, he scored a magnificent solo try - the match-winner, as it happened, for though the 'Cherry and Whites' threw everything into a last desperate rally we held out. Only just, mind you, for by this time Leeds, too, had been reduced to twelve players, prop forward Joe Anderson having been carried off with concussion. With heavy limbs but light hearts we made for the dressing-room, the opinion amongst the boys being that however far we might progress in the competition, we could never expect a harder or more spine-tingling match than Wigan had given us that afternoon. As events were to prove, we were mistaken - vastly so.

Once again the draw was kind to us, for not only were we drawn at home again, but our opponents, Warrington, had twice that winter already fallen fairly facile victims to us in League matches. We had defeated them 32-9 at Headingley and done even better in the return encounter by defeating them 42-7 on their own Wilderspool enclosure - the first occasion since 1937, incidentally, that Leeds had been successful there.

The cup tie, played on a snow-covered ground, was won just as easily as had been the two League encounters, our task being made immeasurably easier by the unfortunate injuries sustained by the three Warrington players, Robin Thompson (fractured shoulder), Frank Wright (concussion), and Alf Arnold (damaged ribs). Robin and Frank were off the field for the whole of the second half, but the plain and (for the 'Wires') sad fact was that the side was but a shadow of the powerful outfits of the seasons just past. It was second-row forward Don Robinson who showed us the way to victory by pouncing on a loose ball and driving it through in a scurry of snow for the first try. I repeated my Stanley Matthews act against Wigan with a long dribble for a try near the posts. Harry Street (two) and Delmos Hodgkinson were the other scorers. I kicked five goals, and we had cleared our second hurdle by twenty-eight points to six.

Who would we draw next, we wondered over the weekend following the Warrington match, and if we had been given the choice out of seven survivors there was one lot of opponents we would have avoided like a plague. Cup draws, however, have no respect for individual preferences; thus it came about that we were faced with the prospect of the journey to Thrum Hall, where the powerful and successful Halifax team looked like providing us with the toughest opposition imaginable. Many thought they would master us. Certainly we would have liked to avoid meeting Halifax until such time as the elimination process offered us no option, but now that the die was cast there was no lack of confidence in the Headingley camp, for if nothing else we had a score of two to settle with the Thrum Hall boys, as a bare twelve months previously they had eliminated us from the competition in the second round and on our own 'midden' at Headingley. The toughness of the opposition raised, as is nearly always the case at 'Big Match' time, suggestions that the Leeds team go away for special training, but authority at Headingley (sensibly, so I consider) believe that the fairly violent transportation from the familiar environment and the inevitable interference with normal training methods have an unsettling effect on a player. Speaking from my own experience, I find my form invariably suffers when I am uprooted suddenly from my normal habits and routine.

The permitted attendance at Thrum Hall was within the region of 27,500, and I am told that Black Market ticket transactions reached a new 'high', though I personally would describe it as a 'low'. Whether it is League or Union, tickets for the 'plum' matches seem to reach the hands of everybody except the people who really matter - the ordinary 'bob' bank supporter who is at his post regularly each Saturday, come fair or foul weather.

I know it is asking a lot that a club should be asked to forfeit ground advantage in an important cup tie, but during the week preceding the Halifax tie - which saw my home and workplace literally besieged by people whom I knew as genuine Rugby League supporters - I could not help wishing that the real 'crowd-pulling' matches were not staged at Odsal Stadium but on a ground large enough to accommodate a more generous proportion of the thousands so evidently desperate to see them. Be this as it may, however, Thrum Hall was filled to capacity as we lined up as follows:

Halifax: Owen; Asquith, Daniels, Dean, Freeman; Broadhurst, Kielty; Thorley, Ackerley, Wilkinson, Pearce, Clift, Traill.
Leeds: Quinn; Hodgkinson, McLellan, Jones, Broughton; Lendill, Stevenson; Anderson, Prior, Hopper, Poole, Robinson, Street.

It was in a way quite a gathering of the clans, this Leeds-Halifax cup tie, for alongside me in the Leeds side was my fellow Ernie Hopper (Maesteg), whilst Halifax included no fewer than five Welshmen - Garfield Owen (Newport), Harper Daniels (Llanelly), John Freeman (Cardiff), John Thorley (Neath), and Les Pearce (Swansea). Countrymen or not, we never have either time or opportunity for the social graces on these occasions, and this was no exception. From the evidence of the first couple of scrums, it was crystal clear that fratricide rather than fraternity was to be the general rule. There were five penalty kicks awarded in as many minutes, and in the same period Referee Appleton had occasion to speak to four players. Nerves, indeed, were bow-string taut in those early stages, and not surprisingly perhaps (for Leeds anyway) they snapped - we were penalized for a play-the-ball infringement inside our own twenty-five. Garfield Owen kicked a grand goal from the touchline. Within minutes I was presented (that is the *mot juste*) with a chance to do likewise but, to my horror and dismay, missed from bang in front of the posts. Worse still I missed another only slightly more difficult shot a minute or two later, and this squandering of opportunities was certainly not doing the morale of the side any good.

That's the way it looked as the rampant Halifax forwards penned us in our own quarter, and our hopes sank to zero as

Ken Traill in his own typical style charged over our goal-line with three blue-and-ambered figures draped around his ample shoulders. It was 5-0 to Halifax, and in next to no time 10-0, and the Thrum Hall supporters were really in ecstasies as Traill again thrust his way over for a splendid try after he had side-stepped three opponents with the practised poise of a Test three-quarter. Garfield Owen converted this one, and with only twenty minutes gone our hopes of Wembley were dying.

I have referred to the Headingley team spirit earlier in this book, and certainly it was to stand us in good stead at Thrum Hall. With Keith McLellan repeatedly urging, coaxing and cajoling them on, the lads began to take a grip on things and with Bernard Prior winning the strike in three vital scrums we gradually worked our way upfield. From a penalty awarded for another play-the-ball infringement, I was able to atone for previous misses by sending one plumb between the posts. Hardly had the last Leeds cheer subsided when Bernard Poole - what a hero he so often was for Leeds - worked Jack Lendill away from a play-the-ball and the off-half ran cleverly to leave Traill and Garfield Owen flat-footed on his way to the posts. My kick was on the mark and, with half-time on us, we were, thank goodness, back in the game with a real fighting chance.

The second session had hardly resumed before Kielty was penalized for feeding his own forwards in a scrum near the twenty-five, and I was grateful for the 'gift'. Only one point in it now but Halifax, with their strong forward rushes, repeatedly rocked us on our none-too-sprightly heels and once Harper Daniels gave us a deadly fright with a wonderful burst half the length of the field which was only stopped at the corner flag. It was hard, dour stuff, with Halifax clinging on grimly to their one-point lead and Leeds striving desperately to overtake them. The tension mounted with the fleeting minutes and now it was Halifax who cracked. Another play-the-ball infringement gave us a penalty kick a few yards in from the touchline, just outside their twenty-five. I've kicked much harder ones, but none which has so terrified me by thoughts of the consequences of failure.

It is, I admit, fortunate that I do not by habit spend much time over the preliminaries of place-kicking, otherwise I'm sure I'd have missed this one in my preoccupation with the prize at stake. As it happened, my kick soared straight and true, and as I watched it go I remember thinking 'Now we're for it', anticipating of course that within the short period left for play those Halifax forwards would make a really supreme effort to snatch the game out of the fire. Yet oddly enough it was our own chaps who seemed to derive the incentive, and in the very last minute of the game Harry Street and young Del Hodgkinson combined brilliantly on the flank and an inside pass from Del sent Keith McLellan careering fifty yards to the side of the posts. My kick was a formality this time, and Leeds were through to the semi-final. In the dressing-room afterwards our theme song, 'We'll keep right on to the end of the Road', rang out loud and clearly.

Our semi-final opponents proved to be the Cumberland team Whitehaven, and the venue decided upon Odsal Stadium, Bradford, where Warrington had ousted us in our last semi-final appearance two years previously. With wins over strong combinations like Wigan and Halifax to our credit, we were naturally confident over the outcome of the Whitehaven match. It proved to be the hardest - certainly the most thrilling - of them all. The Cumbrians had no pretensions to class but my word how they could cover and tackle, and although we enjoyed for most of the game a 2-1 advantage from the scrums, only on two occasions was our back division allowed to work the ball wingwards with its usual precision and fluency. Fortunately for us, George Broughton was in top form on the left wing and twice he hurtled in at the corner flag in the best Drew Turnbull manner after Bernard Poole had accomplished the spadework.

This was Whitehaven's first semi-final appearance and they quickly showed that the occasion hadn't overawed them, for within two minutes of the kick-off they were ahead with a penalty goal kicked from thirty-five yards by full-back John McKeown. He's a wonderful place-kicker - one can almost shout 'coconut' every time he shies at the sticks - and at Odsal he surpassed himself for not only did he add another penalty from four yards inside his own half of the field but followed it up with an absolutely magnificent conversion of the Whitehaven try scored by McMenememy. With a narrow angle, and a strong wind to contend with, McKeown steered it plumb between the posts and Odsal rose to him, as well they might. This superb goal gave the Cumbrians a 9-8 lead, for just previously I had kicked a goal to add to George Broughton's tries.

With half an hour to go, it was anybody's match. We, of course, were desperately anxious that it should be 'ours', and went all out for the score that would clinch the issue our way. Whitehaven were equally determined to hold on to their one-point lead and, although still out-hooked in the scrums, never conceded an inch that didn't have to be fought for. Indeed the tight and unyielding quality of the Cumbrian defence may be better appreciated by recording the fact that at one period they retained the ball in thirty-nine successive play-the-ball movements.

As you may guess, we in the Leeds back division endured agonies of frustration as the minutes ticked away, with Whitehaven retaining not only their slender lead but for much of the time the ball as well. There were other agonies, too, the physical agony of our periodic encounters with our hard-tackling adversaries, but these we were prepared to suffer gladly if we could but find the one chink in the defensive armour that confronted us.

'Stevo', Jack Lendill, then Keith McLellan, then myself, one and all we tried to find the gap that would send George Broughton or Del Hodgkinson haring for the goal-line, but there were no gaps in this wonderful Whitehaven defence, and with the clock showing a mere five minutes left for play it looked as though the Odsal Stadium was once again to be our hoodoo ground.

Nothing daunted, however, the Leeds forwards gathered (from goodness knows where) the energy for one last assault, and as three Whitehaven defenders buried Joe Anderson in the tackle thirty-odd yards from their posts the burly prop forward managed to whip out a pass to Jeff Stevenson. Before a man on either side could even guess at his intention, 'Stevo' had dropped a superb goal. It was a typical 'Stevo' effort - brilliant, absolutely unexpected, and a match-winner. We were done with Whitehaven, and heartily glad we were to be so; for us now the haven of the Odsal dressing-rooms where we toasted little Jeff in bottled beer until the mud was almost dry on our spattered shorts and jerseys.

There was music, too, and appropriately enough its provider was 'Stevo', who had borrowed Geoff Gunney of Hunslet's portable gramophone for the occasion. Inevitably, of course, the record played was the 'End of the Road'. We were indeed at the very last milestone - Wembley - and even to think of it was to forget all the heartaches, the bruises, and the mental tension encountered *en route*.

16

ROAD'S END

The semi-final at Odsal had been played on the last Saturday of March, which meant that there was a whole month's interval before we were due to oppose Barrow at Wembley.

In ordinary circumstances this would have imposed a heavy strain not only on the players but even more so perhaps on those charged with the task of keeping them up to concert pitch both physically and mentally. Argue as you like, there is no gainsaying that a succession of ordinary League matches sandwiched in between the semi-final and final do unmistakably produce a feeling of anti-climax amongst players who have been keyed up to great tension.

It helped us, I suppose, and indeed our opponents too, that we both possessed an opportunity of figuring in the Championship play-off semi-finals. This meant that we had to strive at concert pitch for every match throughout the month of April. As I've mentioned earlier, however, the Headingley approach to vital matches is pre-eminently sane and sensible; indeed, not even the Cup Final was allowed to disturb our normal routine. We did not travel down to our Final H.Q., the Aldenham Lodge Hotel, Radlett, until the Friday morning before the match, and I'm certain we benefited mentally by the fact that we were spared the business of adapting ourselves to strange surroundings, food, and atmosphere, at what was a pretty tense time for all of us.

In striving to create the all-essential feeling of normality, the Headingley authorities produced a psychological master-stroke in permitting, at the club's expense, wives and girl friends to travel to London with the team. Certainly we as players appreciated this gesture, and it did us a power of good to know that the girls were there to watch us and to share in the celebration - or commiserations - with us when it was all over. Ken Dalby produced his own master-stroke during the week preceding the Big Match by ensuring that our final practice session took place on a similarly heavily grassed surface to that which we would encounter on the Stadium itself. At Headingley, as with most grounds on which we'd played during the past month, the surface was bone hard and dusty, so as part of the acclimatization process we travelled out the mile to Kirkstall where we enjoyed a profitable work-out on a lush green surface.

The Saturday before the Final we had lost to Oldham in the Championship semi-final, but this defeat did not undermine our confidence, though it had added to the Headingley casualty list, for in addition to Joe Anderson, who had missed seven matches with a dislocated shoulder, and Del Hodgkinson, who had missed four with a strained ankle, we now had Don Robinson (wrist injury), Keith McLellan (cut eye), and George Broughton (cut ear) reporting daily for treatment. Happily, however, all were passed fit to travel down to London, though had we but known it Robbie's wrist injury was in actual fact a fracture and it was only as a result of a top secret conference with Ken Dalby that he played at all. Ken in fact left the final decision to Robbie, and by golly he must be still blessing the day he did so, for the giant second-row forward proved a tower of strength at Wembley.

In contrast to Barrow who kept their boys in suspense until the very last moment, Ken Dalby named the Leeds XIII on the Monday before the match. It was the side that had defeated Whitehaven in the semi-final: Pat Quinn; Del Hodgkinson, Keith McLellan (capt.), Lewis Jones, George Broughton; Jack Lendill, Jeff Stevenson; Joe Anderson, Bernard Prior, Ernie Hopper, Bernard Poole, Don Robinson, Harry Street.

I will not claim that this was the greatest XIII ever to represent the famous Headingley club, but it was at least a *team* in the true sense of that sometimes much-abused word. We played an attacking brand of rugby and, moreover, played it collectively with a fine appreciation of each other's strengths and weaknesses, whilst our team spirit forged in the heat of the hard and fiercely competitive League and Cup battles was really something to reckon with. Then in the twenty-seven-year-old Australian Keith McLellan, who had been recommended to the Leeds club by that peerless centre three-quarter of other days, Frank O'Rourke, we had a captain who inspired those around him by personal example as well exhortation. I can pay Keith McLellan no greater compliment than to say that with him alongside at centre in the Leeds team I derived the same kind of encouragement and inspiration as I used to get from the great Jack Matthews during my start as a Rugby Union international.

At full-back we had the former England Rugby Union international and British Lion centre three-quarter, Pat

King of Rugger

Quinn, who had settled in brilliantly to his new position and the thirteen-a-side game. As becomes a former three-quarter, Pat was adept at linking up with his threes. As far as the League game is concerned, this is 'just what the doctor ordered'. On the wings were eighteen-year-old Delmos Hodgkinson, who was bidding for a coveted Cup-winner's medal in his very first season as a professional, and George Broughton, a son of a former international who was one of the several Leeds schools' players on the Headingley books. Both Del and George could shift along the touchline, and Del in fact had notched twenty-seven tries in his first season - many of them the product of a nifty side-step. In the centre were Keith McLellan and myself, at stand-off half Jack Lendill, another product of Leeds schoolboy rugby.

Jack as a matter of fact supplied welcome copy for the newspaper boys, for he was the one Leeds player who had actually been taught at school by Ken Dalby before the latter relinquished schoolmastering for the job of managing Leeds. Another copy-making angle was the fact that Jack had emigrated to Australia with his family, and had returned to try his luck as a professional. Angles apart, however, Jack Lendill was a cracking good stand-off half, as indeed he had to be to displace World Cup player Gordon Brown in the side. Partnering Lendill was the inimitable 'Stevo' - I say 'inimitable' because if you judged Rugby League players in the same way as the American Press boys assess the boxing fraternity then you might open your newspaper one day to read 'Stevo' described as 'pound for pound' the finest footballer in the game.

Jeff's weight - nine stone odd 'soaking wet' - was the subject of a good many quips and wisecracks in the Headingley dressing-room, but it (or the lack of it) never placed him at a disadvantage against anyone. He was a brilliant natural footballer; elusive as they come, a master of the unexpected, and a great man to have on your side when the going was toughest. Like Del Hodgkinson and George Broughton, 'Stevo' had developed via the Leeds schools and the Headingley 'Nursery', and had played for the R.A.F. in service representative matches.

The fact that Jeff was at scrum half was, I might tell you, purely a matter of team expediency, for if circumstances had required it he could have played at stand-off with equal skill, poise, and assurance. In the front row of the scrum we had my fellow countryman Ernie Hopper who, at 6ft. 4in. and 15st.8lb., was the tallest and heaviest man in the side, Joe Anderson, another fifteen-stoner from Castleford, and between them a local lad, Bernard Prior, who all season had been making some of the League's hooking top sawyers sit up and take notice. In the second row were the fabulous Don Robinson and Bernard Poole - a perfectly blended pair. Robinson was tremendously strong and a great grafter and Poole the complete all-round forward ever looking for a chance to exploit his rocket burst and famous wide pass. At loose forward we had Harry Street, former Test player and still at twenty-nine years of age one of the very best in the business.

Barrow, who like Leeds had a long and formidable record in the Challenge Cup competition, brought on their heads a great deal of criticism by delaying their final team selection until the eve of the game, and there was even louder criticism when it was found that the Selectors had omitted the former Wigan prop forward Frank Barton. Had he been selected he would have been appearing in his fifth post-war final - a record. As it was, Barrow, with seven of their thirteen past the thirty mark, banked heavily on experience, and I confess they looked a formidable outfit by any standard.

In their stand-off half and captain Willie Horne they had

a strategist of infinite guile and vast experience, whilst Phil Jackson, at twenty-four years of age, was probably the most complete footballing centre three-quarter in the Rugby League, if not also in both amateur and professional codes combined. On the wings, too, they had pace and craft, for the years seemingly had left both Jim Lewthwaite and Frank Castle untouched where these virtues were concerned. Then there was the pack - a strong compact unit containing brilliant individuals like Don Wilson, Jack Grundy, and the giant George Woosey. We respected them heartily, I can assure you.

We passed the Saturday morning of the Final quietly playing golf at the Porter's Park Golf Club, and for three of the side at least - 'Stevo', Pat Quinn, and myself - it promised to be a lucky day. 'Stevo', having hit the 'jack-pot' on the club's fruit machine on his first go, landed a prize of a box of golf balls which he promptly split between the team's two golfing members, Pat Quinn and myself. A few hours later we were at the Stadium, and there to greet me were my brothers, Alun and Cliff, who always contrive to be present for the most important matches I'm engaged in. As we chatted and exchanged family gossip, my thoughts raced down the years to that January afternoon of 1950 at Twickenham when I played my first match for Wales. Alun and Cliff were there, too, and I could not help but wonder whether history was going to repeat itself by making my first appearance in London as a Rugby League player as memorable an occasion as my first Rugby Union international.

At last the Big Moment had arrived, or nearly so, for as we trooped out in double file - Leeds in their blue and amber strip and Barrow resplendent in their special Final outfits of bright scarlet jerseys with a white 'V' - it was to face the nerve-racking preliminary inseparable from the Wembley occasion. First the teams were introduced to the Rugby League's President, the Rt. Hon. The Earl of Derby, and then followed the anthem played by the massed bands of the Coldstream, Scots, Irish, and Welsh Guards.

For me and, as I subsequently discovered, for my Leeds colleagues too, they were quite the longest and most nerve-racking five minutes of my career. It is difficult to explain the feeling, but standing there immobile in the middle of the vast green desert that is the Empire Stadium, Wembley, it seems as though for the first time in your career you've been pitchforked into an atmosphere of absolute strangeness and unnaturalness. The magnitude of the place seems to weigh you down, makes you feel pathetically small, and somehow inadequate. I comforted myself with the thought that nerves, as always, would disappear the very moment the ball was in motion.

But Wembley must be different from all other grounds in actuality as well as in imagination, for with all of us, both Leeds and Barrow players, the anxiety complex was to last the full ninety minutes, and I'm now well able to understand why it so often is that the Cup Final fails to live up to expectations from the purely technical aspect.

Speaking from a Leeds point of view, I'm perfectly sure that had we exploited our favourite attacking manoeuvre - the wide pass - during the first half when we were very definitely on top, then we would have crossed over leading by more than the three points which was the actual margin. I am prepared to admit that Barrow, too, in all probability excluded one or two of their normal tactical gambits in the interests of safety. It all illustrates the manner in which Wembley nerves affect the Finalists. Personally, I'd welcome the chance to play in this Barrow-Leeds Final all over again, if only to establish whether one feels the same way twice.

As I write this book in the quiet atmosphere of my own

home at Leeds, far from the scene of conflict, I could kick myself now for the caution that caused me to neglect opportunity at Wembley. Maybe twenty-five other players are feeling exactly the same way.

The teams were:

Leeds: Quinn; Broughton, Jones, McLellan, Hodgkinson; Lendill, Stevenson; Anderson, Prior, Hopper, Poole, Robinson, Street.
Barrow: Ball; Lewthwaite, Jackson, Rea, Castle; Horne, Harris; Woosey, Redhead, Parker, Grundy, Healey, Wilson.

It was Barrow who took the offensive at the kick-off, but not for long, however, for a penalty enabled us to relieve the pressure and for ten minutes or so play hovered near the half-way line with neither side able to establish any clear-cut advantage. As the minutes ticked by we seemed to be obtaining a very definite edge on our opponents. We were winning the scrums and our backs were certainly looking dangerous when in possession. If this had been an ordinary League match, I'm convinced we would have had a least six or nine points in the bag before half-time, but we were edgy and nervous, which meant that our passing lacked its usual fluency. In addition, we were constantly wary of trying anything that might be conducive to error. Yet even so there were a couple of near misses; once I was nailed by Billy Horne within sight of the corner flag and then 'Stevo' spreadeagled the defence with a typical break only for the final pass (mine) to go astray. I missed a penalty during this period too - not a particularly easy one, but neither could it be described as difficult in comparison with many of the shots I'd put over in this my record-breaking year.

Our forwards were going great guns at this stage. 'Stevo' was playing to them brilliantly and his perfect understanding with loose forward Harry Street must assuredly have been hard on the nerves of the Barrow defenders. It was a move by 'Stevo' and Harry that entrenched us in the Barrow twenty-five, and once there our forwards commenced to pound away at the goal-line with a sustained power and urgency that had the crowd roaring for minutes on end. First Street, then Poole, then Hopper, and in turn every one of those blue-and-amber-jerseyed forwards were hauled down within inches of the goal-line, and strong, compact and courageous as was our opponents' tackling and covering, this incessant battering was bound, we thought, sooner or later to produce a dent.

The man who did the cracking was, as it happened, Pat Quinn who, with the instinctive footballer's appreciation of the situation, intervened in a play-the-ball movement to take a short pass from Bernard Prior and fairly hurl himself through the slim gap his keen eyes had detected in the defence. Pat was held momentarily en route, but 13 and a half stone on the burst takes a lot of stopping and he was able to ground the ball to a roar that must have been heard back at Headingley. My kick alas was sadly adrift, but the important thing was that we had drawn first blood in a Wembley Final, and taking inspiration from the knowledge the lads kept piling on the pressure. It was only fractional errors on our part and full-blooded tackling by the Barrow side that prevented us increasing the lead, and once after a drive that produced the 'action shot' of the season George Broughton hit the corner flag to deny us what looked a certain score. Then almost on half-time we had a shock when Jim Lewthwaite forced a way over in the corner following an unexpected Barrow breakaway. Luckily for us, however, referee Appleton's whistle signalled a 'knock-on' and we breathed again.

'Don't forget the switch,' was Ken Dalby's parting injunction to us as we came out for the second half. Nor did we. From the very first scrum we exploited the manoeuvre we had trained so assiduously to bring to perfection on practice nights back at Headingley. It worked like a charm. Jack Lendill hared left from the scrum with all Barrow eyes following him, meanwhile I ran right from the left-centre position to take 'Stevo's' streamlined pass. Phil Jackson, Billy Horne, and Johnny Rea were all left high and dry by the speed and unexpectedness of the movement, and with all Wembley seemingly yawning before me I slipped a pass out to Del Hodgkinson, who went forty-five yards like a 'Derby' favourite coming down the final straight to leave full-back Ball literally standing with a side-step that was vintage 'Alun Edwards'. The crowd fairly rose to that one, but so likewise did Barrow, for now we began to feel the full impact of that powerful packs as they thundered in phalanx downfield, whilst behind them the cagey Billy Horne began to dictate the trend of the game with his shrewd passing and punting. It was Horne who put them back in the game with a penalty goal, and it was Horne who inspired almost every one of the whole series of all-out assaults they now launched on our goal-line.

It was our turn to tackle now, and they had us full stretch for a quarter of an hour on end. Yet just when it seemed as if Barrow must score again, it was Leeds who did so. By a stroke of real rugby irony, the man responsible was Jack Grundy who had been playing like two men in the Barrow second row, and I'm sure he must still be kicking himself for falling for one of the oldest dodges in the game. In a general mix up near his own goal-line Jack reacted instinctively to what he thought was a shout from a colleague and whipped the ball back swiftly but, alas for his side, rather more wildly than the circumstances permitted, and worse still, the 'colleague' proved to be none other than Leeds' fifteen-stone second-row forward Don Robinson. 'Robbie' is a hard man to stop near the line at any time, but now with a cup winner's medal, not to mention a £40 pay day, in the offing it would have taken all the steel plate in Barrow's shipyard to stop him. Johnny Rea and Jim Lewthwaite were courageous men, and they both crashed into 'Robbie', but the giant Leeds forward barely faltered in his stride before he crashed over the line with the two draped about his person.

Nine-two to Leeds and the Cup seemed ours for the taking. Yet Barrow were far from done with, and spearheaded by the matchless Billy Horne they pulled out all the stops in an effort to overtake us.

From his own half of the field Billy engineered a move that sent the big prop forward Reg Parker galloping into our half, where he passed to Phil Jackson. Phil, who had been chafing at the bit throughout the afternoon, had at long last a chance to show his paces, which meant of course that all that we saw was the flash of his metal-studded heels as he stepped out of George Broughton's tackle and hared off upfield, producing *en route* that matchless swerve of his to round Pat Quinn and 'Robbie'. A great try and one which Bill Horne converted. This meant that with twenty minutes to go the game was wide open.

Much, of course, has already been said and written of Barrow's great second-half rally, but while I'll agree that they had the better of the play during that period I shall never subscribe to the view that Leeds were fortunate to hold out. A team that had played as well as Leeds did during the first half were surely entitled to the honours; not only that, when Billy Horne's boys gained their second-half ascendancy, the Leeds tackling was the very last word in efficiency and finality.

Keith McLellan and diminutive 'Stevo' performed near miracles in this direction, yet the game was to end with an incident as controversial afterwards as it was thrilling and dramatic at the time. It happened in the very last minute and its cause was surprisingly Billy Horne, who managed to get his young centre, Johnny Rea, away from a scrum practically on our own line. Johnny ran strongly through or tiring defence until he was almost up to our twenty-five, where he elected to kick towards the corner flag. In a pretty desperate race for the flag George Broughton got there just ahead of Frank Castle and a whole bevy of red and white jerseys - and Barrow's last chance had gone.

The 1957 Cup Final was now, of course, all over bar the shouting, and there was sure plenty of that, for as the thousands-strong Leeds contingent revelled in London far into the night their Barrow counterparts were busy discussing the 'ifs' and 'buts' of Johnny Rea's dramatic last-minute burst. The general opinion (shared by a large section of the National Press) was that if Johnny had passed out to his wing-man Frank Castle in preference to kicking ahead, then Barrow must assuredly have won. Jim Sullivan was one of those who subscribed to the view that Castle would have scored had he received the ball, and Frank himself evidently thought so too, for in a Press interview afterwards he is quoted as saying: 'I moved behind Johnny to go inside him. I wanted to have all the Leeds line to go at. I was shouting for the ball all the time.' As for Johnny Rea's version, he said: 'I looked over my shoulder for Frank, but could only see a Leeds player on my heels. I looked to my right and could see no one with me. Jones was coming across so I kicked. I could hear nothing but the roar of the crowd.'

My own view is - and it is the view subscribed to by the Leeds players on the spot - that young Rea did absolutely the right thing under the circumstances for although his burst had originally taken the Leeds defence unawares we had recovered quickly and I am certain that I would have closed with, and grassed, the Barrow centre before he had travelled many yards further. Pat Quinn, who had Frank Castle in his sights over every yard he'd travelled alongside Rea, had called out, 'O.K., Lew, I'll take Castle.' Possibly Pat's confident call induced the comparatively inexperienced Rea to kick sooner than he had intended, but soon or late I'm certain that the kick ahead was the right and in fact the only answer to the problem that Johnny Rea had to solve in a split second of high drama. You'll never of course convince Barrow men that this was indeed the case, and I for one will never blame them. Their opinions I'm sure were as honestly conceived as our own. Indeed, no praise is too high to bestow on these Lancashire footballers for the manner in which they took their defeat - there had been no questionable tactics employed on the field, and there were certainly no hard words off it.

I only wish that some of the people who imagine that professional rugger is a game for thugs and mercenaries could have been there to see the Barrow lads clamouring to offer their congratulations to Keith McLellan when it was all over. Keith, incidentally, presented quite a spectacle as he held the Challenge Cup aloft supported by the shoulders of the lads. Blood was running down his cheek as a result of an eye gash he'd received against Oldham in the previous Saturday's semi-final having been re-opened. The sight of him called to mind the school day history book pictures of the wounded hero returning home from the wars, and come to that Keith had surely been one of the side's great heroes throughout the campaign. In the Final, as in the other rounds, he had got through a vast amount of hard, unobtrusive toil. Whether it was a case of tackle, a burst down the middle, or 'guts', wholeheartedness revealed themselves in every facet of Keith's football playing, and they were without a doubt qualities that acted as an inspiration to his colleagues.

King of Rugger

To Jeff Stevenson went the additional honour of the 'Lance Todd' memorial trophy, as the outstanding player of the day, and richly did he deserve it, for Wembley had seen little 'Stevo' at his brilliant best. During the first half, when Leeds held the ascendancy, his speed, dexterity, and lighting forays from the base of the scrum kept the Barrow defence at full stretch, and during the second period, when our opponents were on top, his magnificent covering and tigerish tackling sustained us in some pretty desperate situations. Don Robinson, too, had played the game of a lifetime, and I imagine that it must have taken oceans of liniment to soothe the bruises of those Barrow players who had encountered the full impetus of his battering-ram rushes from the play-the-ball movements and the rucks. Eighteen-year-old Del Hodgkinson was another who enjoyed a memorable Final. He was the youngest player afield, but no one would have thought so from the poise and assurance with which he grasped his one great opportunity.

Everyone in the Leeds side, save possibly myself, could feel well satisfied with their achievements at Wembley. Not that I was all that disappointed with my own effort. Naturally I would have like to have kicked my goals and, as I said earlier been given an opportunity of playing the match all over again. Still, the important thing was that it had been a *team* success, and with due modesty I claimed to have fulfilled my allotted part even though I did not produce the spectacular stuff many people apparently expected.

It was now indeed, at long last, really the 'End of the Road', but the thrills and excitement were by no means over, and indeed those that were left were all the sweeter for the fact that they were enjoyed in an atmosphere of absolute content and relaxation. First there was the celebration get-together with our wives and friends after the match, and then the tremendous welcome awaiting us back at Leeds on the Sunday evening. Thousands lined the Town Hall Square to cheer us as we cruised the city in an open coach. We were given a civic reception by Alderman T. A. Jessop, the Lord Mayor of Leeds. His Worship, incidentally, was a keen Hunslet supporter, but I'm certain that neither his civic or sporting pride were any the less for the fact that the Challenge Cup reposed at Headingley rather than Parkside.

My first (but I hope not the last) visit to Wembley had been a tremendous experience and I feel that I look back on it as such mainly because I was fortunate enough to have been on the winning side there. It must be the bitterest pill of all to lose at the Stadium after riding on the crest of a continuous wave of success throughout the months that have gone before. Barrow, as I've remarked, took their defeat in the most sporting spirit imaginable, but I'm quite sure that privately every one of them must have felt that the bottom had fallen out of their world.

As a matter of fact I broke off writing this chapter to watch Manchester United and Bolton Wanderers in the 1958 F.A. Cup Final on television, and when it was all over a whole twelve months seemed but yesterday. Mentally, at any rate, I was back once more at the Stadium. I could well imagine how gloriously happy those Bolton boys were feeling as they danced around Nat Lofthouse as he held the cup aloft, but it must have been so different for the Manchester lads. Mention of the United will ever echo the terrible tragedy of Munich. It was a tragedy that shocked the whole world.

My own personal grief, too, was deeper for the fact that many of those who died at Munich were friends of mine dating back to happy days on the sea front at Blackpool, where both the United and the British Rugby League Test side were undergoing special training for a cup tie and an international match respectively. Indeed, whether established star or 'Babe', they didn't come any better than these United boys.

17

MY GREATEST SEASON

On August 22nd, 1956, against Bradford Northern at Odsal Stadium, I scored three tries and kicked eleven goals - thirty-one points in all - to set up a new individual match record for the Leeds club.

It was the third match of the new season, and had I but known it my achievement at Odsal was the forerunner of several others that between them, numerically at any rate, were to provide me with my greatest season in Rugby League; perhaps in any type of rugby. Certainly I never dreamed on that August evening at Odsal that I should be the player to surpass the great Jim Sullivan's all-time Rugby League record of 432 points in a single season. Jim's record had in fact remained untouched for almost a quarter of a century for it was in the season 1933-4, at the zenith of his great career as Wigan's full-back, that he had kicked his 204 goals, and scored eight tries to create a record that I for one never expected to see approached, much less surpassed.

162

Still, the target was there for anyone to aim at and I suppose anything can happen in rugby football. Indeed, plenty of pleasant things were happening to me at Headingley.

Leeds, to begin with, had got off to a fine start and scoring opportunities were accordingly plentiful. Before August was out I had sixty-five points in the bag including my haul at Bradford. September, too, proved a successful month, for by kicking six goals apiece against Dewsbury and York and another seven against Warrington I brought my tally up to 128. During October the transition to muddy grounds and a heavier ball retarded my progress somewhat and I could manage no more than thirty-two. November was slightly better with thirty-seven - a hat trick of tries against Keighley helping to swell the total - whilst December, with its extra Christmas match, earned me another fifty-six points.

Thus at the turn of the year, with twenty-five matches played, my grand total of points scored stood at 243, and assuming Leeds reached the final at Wembley, the Championship Final, and that I was selected to play in the three Rugby League Test matches against France, I had twenty-seven matches in which to score the 189 points necessary to overhaul Sullivan. Not that I gave the matter serious thought at the time, for quite honestly my sights, like those of the rest of the Leeds team, were fixed more on appearances in the Cup and Championship Finals. Even to those statistically minded followers who had considered that matter it seemed unlikely that I could get anywhere near Jim's goals tally, since I'd only kicked ninety-six in twenty-five matches, and with no thought that I could bang over another 108 in the second half of the season.

The New Year, however, opened with a real bang for me, and in the very first match against Hull I was able to score two tries and land five goals. The next match against

King of Rugger

Warrington brought me another hat trick of tries, the match with St Helens a try and five goals, and to crown a marvellous start to the year 1957 the First Test against France at Headingley saw me score twenty-one points - a try and nine goals in a 45-12 win for Great Britain. I now had over 300 points in the kitty and saw the possibility, fantastic as it still seemed, of overhauling Sullivan's points record.

February, with its cup ties with Wigan and Warrington and League encounters with Huddersfield, York, and Castleford, was even more successful, for I averaged exactly a dozen points a match to bring my total up to 362. They were certainly hectic days, these; not only were Leeds in the middle of an inspired League run but the club were in addition going great guns in the Cup, and what with my being only seventy points short of the all-time record the newspaper boys were seldom short of copy. Where goal-kicking was concerned I could hardly go wrong at this period of my career, and indeed the chances are that if I'd turned my hand to card-playing at this juncture I must have accumulated a sizable sum of money, for in four consecutive games during the month of March - Great Britain against France, Leeds against Halifax, Wakefield and Bradford respectively - I reeled off a 'nap' hand of five goals on each occasion. Three tries and an additional three goals shared between matches against Whitehaven and Hull gave me a tally of fifty-five for the whole month.

With my points total for whole season standing high, and with our entry to the Challenge Cup Final assured (if only just) as a result of the Whitehaven game, I now had to agree that I had a great chance of making my own bit of Rugby League history.

A tight match with Wakefield Trinity, in which I managed to put over three goals, brought my score up to 426 - and now coincidence entered the business in the most odd and tantalising manner imaginable.

I needed just seven points - a try and a couple of goals - to pass Jim Sullivan's figure, and the first opportunity which presented itself after the Wakefield match was of all places (fate must have its own stage manager) St. Helens, where the man in charge was none other than the record-holder himself. It would indeed have made a nice story had I been able to annex those seven points before the admiring eye of my fellow countryman, but all I actually got at St Helens was the 'bird' from the crowd - and deservedly so, for nothing would go right for me that afternoon and I missed some real 'sitters' from bang in front of the posts. Worse still, more so in view of our Cup Final prospects, Leeds minus prop forward Joe Anderson were properly 'clobbered' by a fine 'Saints' side; 3-44 was the final score, and I most certainly could hardly care less about records, past, present, or future. Even the fates relented, however, for on April 10th, a brief four days after the *débacle*, I was back once more at St Helens as a member of the British side for the Third and final Test with France. Once again Jim Sullivan was sitting on the trainer's bench, this time to see me take the record with five goals and a simple try to take my tally to 440 points.

Naturally I was pleased and it was pleasant to wake up the following morning - my twenty-fifth birthday - and read all the nice things the newspapers had to say of my achievement. What rather took the gilt off things was the arguing and occasional bickering as to whether mine or Big Jim's had been the more praiseworthy performance.

Jim himself, who was one of the first to congratulate me, later went on record as saying: 'It's a fine achievement by Lewis but I don't think you can compare his points total with the one I set up in the 1933-4 season. In pre-war days the ball was heavier than it is now. You really had to kick the ball hard to score. Also there are a lot more penalties awarded in present-day football.' Possibly he (Jim) was right at that, not that I think it matters either way for quite frankly I see nothing wonderful in being able to steer a rugby ball, more so a stationary one, between a pair of uprights. One has, of course, to put in a large amount of practice at the start, but the major part of it is a gift. You either have the natural ability or you have not and, speaking for myself, there are (even in rugby football) other gifts which I would covet far more. Certainly I would prefer to be regarded as a real rugby footballer in the all-round sense, than to be looked upon as a mere place-kicker - however expert. That is why I failed to see the point (save academically) of all the arguments and comparisons, for believe me I was far prouder of the thirty-seven tries I eventually scored that season than the 197 goals I was credited with. Indeed, the best that can be said for the goals, as far as I'm concerned, is that they helped my club to enjoy a great and memorable season. People often ask me what it feels like to the holder of this record or that, and if I am invariably unable to give a satisfactory answer it is because there really isn't one.

Occasionally perhaps, in one of my rare introspective moods, I feel a sense of amazement that fate has singled me out to be the owner of records and achievements that have been beyond the attainment of some of the greatest players rugby football has ever known, but I can assure readers that I do not 'live' with the statistical details of my career. Certainly they do not give me the same inward glow of satisfaction as I derive from the knowledge that I have played a real 'blinder' in an important match.

I suffer, too, from no delusion that any of my records are going to last for ever, for even though a total of over 500 points in a single season of Rugby League football may look quite monumental, some day in the near or distant future some player, at present unheard of, is going to get even more lucky breaks than I did and I shall then be an 'also ran' in the record stakes. Certainly when that day comes, and assuming I'm still around, I won't be found subjecting the new record to any comparison or qualifications. I believe it was Don Bradman who once said, 'Swimming records are still broken regularly though the water gets no different' - an admirable philosophy, I think.

Reverting, however, to the actual achievements of 1956-7 - for their recording, I believe, was one of the reasons that inspired my publishers to commission this book - I finished up the season with 505 points in the bag - thirty-seven tries and 197 goals. Thus in one stroke I had become the first Rugby League player to score 500 points in a season and had become also the holder of the individual points scoring record a Rugby League season.

I had failed, however, to pass Jim Sullivan's record of 204 goals in a season - even so the record did not last much longer, for less than a twelve-month later the feat was accomplished by the Oldham full-back, Bernard Ganley - one of the most consistently accurate kickers in the game.

Other records I established during the course of those memorable months between August, 1956, and May, 1957, were as follows.

During the course of the Batley match on Christmas Day, 1956, I reached my thousandth point for the Leeds club which was, according to the record, the quickest thousand in club history. Then on February 27th, 1957, against Castleford I scored a try and kicked four goals, to pass the Leeds club record of 312 points in a season set up by Bert Cook a few years previously. Another of Cook's records had already fallen to me, of course - that of the highest number of points in a match - when I netted my bag of thirty-one against Bradford Northern early in the season. Finally by the end of the campaign I had accumulated for Leeds 1,526 points during my four and a half seasons with them, which meant that I had passed the records of the Australian, Eric Harris (1,205 points in nine seasons), and that of New Zealand's Bert Cook (1,169 points in six seasons).

I was reminded that there were still a couple of Leeds records that needed passing. One, Joe Thompson's monumental total of 1,883 points during the eleven seasons he played for the club, two, the joint achievement of J.H.Potter, E. Pollard, and Bert Cook and myself, who had all kicked twelve goals in a match, plus the unique record of Eric Harris, who had once scored eight tries in a match against Bradford Northern. For what it was worth, in view of the opposition and the opportunities I was offered, I took the club goal-kicking record shortly afterwards with thirteen goals against Blackpool in an evening game at Headingley.

I am told, incidentally, that I threw away a chance in this match to beat the thirty-one points I'd scored in the Bradford match a year earlier, for I had already crossed for a try in addition to kicking the thirteen goals, and I suppose I could have gone over for the deciding try had I not elected to pass to our American trialist, Al Kirkland, on the wing. The newspapers the next morning anyway were good enough to praise me for my unselfishness, but the truth was that in a match in which Leeds had already scored over sixty points I had lost all count of scores, personal or otherwise. Anyhow, for the sake of a single point, it's nice to think that the oddity of a 'Yank in the Rugby League' was rendered even more romantic by the fact that Al was able to grace his debut with a try.

Joe Thompson's record is, I suppose, well within my scope, but this I'm sure is one instance where comparison is justified. Assuming that I am able to pass his record of 1,883 points, Joe's feat must always rank as the greater, if only for the fact that he was a forward. As for even equalling, much less surpassing, the 'Toowoomba Ghost's' feat of scoring eight tries in a major League encounter - well, I don't fancy myself at all.

My head, I can tell you, is in a whirl after coping with a whole chapter of figures and statistics for, beyond being able to work out the difference between 'winning and losing' money, I've never been a great hand at arithmetic.

Mainly for the interest of Rugby Union readers of this book, I might also point out that the history of professional rugby records several rather more incredulous scoring feats than my own. Playing for Wigan in a Rugby League cup tie against Flimby and Fothergill during the season 1925, Jim Sullivan landed no fewer than twenty-two goals. Then a Major Holland, playing for Huddersfield against Swinton Park Rangers in 1913, kicked eighteen. Greatest scoring feat of all, however, as far as Rugby League is concerned, was that of the Hull Kingston Rovers three-quarter 'Tich' West who, playing in a Northern Union cup tie against a team called Brookland Rovers, scored eleven tries and kicked ten goals - fifty-three points in all if (and I'm not sure) modern scoring values were in operation during 1905. Then Brian Bevan, Lionel Cooper, and Drew Turnbull notwithstanding, the Rugby League try-scoring record for a single season belongs to the Huddersfield winger Albert Rosenfield, who scored eighty during the season 1913-14.

Finally there is the unique record of the Wigan player, J. Hoey, who, during the season 1932-33, played in forty-one matches and scored in every one of them - his record reading eighty-four goals, twenty-one tries - 231 points in all. Yes, the Rugby League is the place for records, so don't run away with the idea that I've got them all!

18

SETBACKS AND DISAPPOINTMENTS

The worst game of rugby football I can remember playing was not, contrary perhaps to the expectations of my own countrymen, the one I played for Wales at Murrayfield in 1951, but a Test match in which I played for Great Britain against New Zealand at Odsal Stadium in 1955, and that was a real stinker if ever there was one.

I missed my passes, likewise my tackles, and to cap an absolutely abject performance, a whole number of fairly simple goal kicks. I had the 'bird' well and truly from the Bradford crowd that afternoon, but the most shattering comment on my performance was reserved for the end as, with the rest of the Great Britain side, I trudged up the long flight of steps that lead through the packed bank to the Odsal dressing-rooms.

My face, I dare say, was already a faint pink as I made my way up the steps, and I'm sure it became a vivid scarlet when a stentorian and broad Yorkshire voice bellowed out,

'Hey, Jonesy, did tha pay to come in here?' Naturally I wasn't flattered, but neither, if it comes to that, was I really broken-hearted, for if a career in sport teaches you anything, it is to accept the rough with the smooth.

Certainly my own career has not left me short of practice in this respect, because I have probably had as many ups and downs as most. Murrayfield was I suppose my earliest and most forcible reminder that rugby football is not just one bed of roses, and then, as I mentioned earlier on, came the broken arm that at one time looked like putting paid to my professional career almost before it had properly begun. Then in the February of 1954, when I seemed on the point of really establishing myself as a rugby player, I sustained a broken leg during the course of a fairly hectic cup tie at the Boulevard, Hull, and that meant that I played no more rugby that season.

Like the one at Batley, this injury was again a pure accident, but just the same I cannot say that I have particularly happy memories of the Boulevard, for the crowd there are one of the most unreasonably partisan in the whole of the Rugby League, and a constant stream of uninformed barracking directed at the opposing players does not really make for enjoyable matches. I may, perhaps, be a bit jaundiced in my view of Hull, for on their own ground, especially, they are a tough and formidable lot to play against, and their style of play, based on strong forward work, is diametrically opposed to that employed by Leeds. Perhaps indeed that is the real reason I seldom relish playing at the Boulevard.

Continuing, however, on the theme of setbacks, my major disappointment during my career as a professional, and indeed it was a disappointment for almost everyone connected with the Rugby League game in this country, was the British party's failure to retain the World Cup when the competition was staged in Australia in the summer of 1957. This competition was inaugurated in 1954 when the tourney, staged in France, was won in brilliant fashion by a young British team, which included two of my Headingley colleagues - Gordon Brown and Don Robinson (then a Wakefield player). Naturally we had high hopes of retaining the trophy as our party, headed by Rugby League Secretary Bill Fallowfield, left London Airport in the June of 1957. The party incidentally was as follows:

Glyn Moses (St. Helens), Lewis Jones (Leeds), Billy Boston (Wigan), Mike Sullivan (Huddersfield), Phil Jackson (Barrow), Alan Davies (Oldham), Ray Price (Warrington), Austin Rhodes (St. Helens), Jeff Stevenson (Leeds), Eric Ashton (Wigan), Alan Prescott (St. Helens - captain), Sid Little (Oldham), Tom McKinney (St. Helens), Tommy Harris (Hull), Jack Grundy (Barrow), Geoff Gunney (Hunslet), Derek Turner (Oldham), John Whiteley (Hull).

It was on the whole a young contingent, though several of the members were rich in experience. In fact, the only non-international in the party was the St. Helens stand-off half, Austin Rhodes, and he - despite his youth - had already gained a cup winner's medal in the previous season's Wembley Final between St. Helens and Halifax. Glyn Moses, our full-back, and Alan Prescott, our captain and prop forward, made up a St. Helens trio, and both possessed a wealth of experience in the big-time stuff.

Indeed for several seasons Glyn Moses had been regarded as one of the best and most consistent full-backs in the game, and there can be no doubt that had he been able to add goal-kicking to his other qualities, he would have been first choice for Great Britain on more than a mere half-dozen occasions. His club mate, Alan Prescott, was one of the real top sawyers of professional football - an immensely powerful prop forward, an inspiring leader, and withal a vastly experienced footballer, for he had already represented Great Britain on no fewer than twenty-three occasions. Alan, incidentally, began his career as a wing three-quarter for Halifax, and although he later developed into a front-row forward weighing sixteen stone plus, he could still shift when the occasion demanded it, and in this respect I will never forget an effort of his in a Test match against France at Headingley when he ran seventy yards for a try that would have done credit to any wing-man playing.

On the wings, we had the tried and proven Billy Boston of Wigan, making his second trip 'Down Under', and Mike Sullivan of Huddersfield who, at twenty-three years of age, had made a wonderful reputation for himself not only in Rugby League, but also in Rugby Union for, as a member of the R.A.F. side in inter-service matches, he had been a great favourite with the Twickenham crowd.

The party carried three recognised centres, apart from myself, viz. Phil Jackson (Barrow), Eric Ashton (Wigan), and Alan Davies (Oldham) - and any one of the trio would have been a 'must' for most sides. Our number one stand-off half was my fellow countryman, the Warrington player, Ray Price - a wily experienced veteran, commonly regarded as one of the best in the business, whilst the scrum-half position went inevitably to my Leeds club mate Jeff Stevenson, 'inevitably' because 'Stevo' had played some of the finest rugby of his career during the season just ended.

In the front row alongside Alan Prescott we had Sid Little of Oldham, a grand sturdy prop who had obtained four full Great Britain caps, and who, before turning over to the League in 1951, had played a lot of top-class Rugby Union with clubs like the Harlequins, Combined Services, and the R.A.F. The 'hookers' were Tom McKinney (St. Helens), an Irishman who, before joining the League, had played his football with the Scottish Rugby Union club Jedforest, and my compatriot, Tom Harris of Hull, another very experienced player, an expert on the strike, and an exceedingly lively performer in other aspects of forward play as demonstrated by his scoring feats for Hull. Indeed, Tommy must be one of the few hookers who have scored a 'hat trick' of tries in any class of rugby.

In the second row we had power, experience, and youth combined in the persons of Jack Grundy of Barrow and Geoff Gunney of Hunslet, whilst John Whiteley (Hull), a member of the first World Cup team in France, and Derek Turner (Oldham) were the specialist loose forwards. All in all, we were, as I say, confident of our ability to resist the challenges of Australia, France, and New Zealand. And we were not alone in that viewpoint, for on arrival in Australia we found the Sydney bookmakers offering the following odds: 3-1 Great Britain, 5-1 Australia, 8-1 France and New Zealand; odds which the bookmakers obviously felt justified in view of the fact that seven of our party of eighteen had acquired previous experience of Australian conditions.

The first match of the competition, decided on a league and not, as is sometimes believed, on a knock-out basis, was scheduled for Sydney on June 15th, where we were to play France exactly a week after our arrival. In preference to plunging us straightaway into the tense big-match atmosphere of Sydney, our managers, Messrs Bill Fallowfield and Hector Rawson, wisely decided that we should do a full week's preliminary training in the much more tranquil atmosphere of Perth. It looked, too, as though the decision was going to turn out a happy one, for in a run-out against a scratch team of Western Australians reinforced by our reserves, the prospective cup team produced a brand of rugby brilliant and cohesive enough to augur well for our chances against France a week ahead. Meanwhile, reports emanating from Sydney warned us that the French team had impressed tremendously with the speed and precision of the football they had showed in training, and all in all, the 1957 series seemed set to explode with a bang.

As things turned out, however, and before a 60,000 crowd on the Sydney Cricket Ground, we proved much too good for the French, and won by 23-5. The ground was in a deplorable condition after heavy rain, but that did not prevent our fellows from turning in a magnificent exhibition of attacking back play which produced really spectacular tries from Mike Sullivan (two), Billy Boston, Phil Jackson, and a real crackerjack seventy-yard effort from 'Stevo'. Owing to a training injury sustained by Ray Price, I began this match at off-half, but did not stay there long, for after a rather badly cut mouth, as a result of a tackle, I had to move out to the wing. Mike Sullivan took over at stand-off half and right well did he play there. Not that my injury detracted from my own enjoyment of this match, for with the team in such grand all-round form I saw plenty of the ball, even on the wing, and that, together with the fact that I was able to kick four goals, made it a pleasant day all round.

Naturally the Australian critics were tremendously impressed with our performance, with the result that if we were favourites before we were doubly so now, despite the fact that the Australians themselves had on the same day triumphed fairly easily over New Zealand at Brisbane by 25-5. We were reckoned to have the edge on them, particularly behind the scrum. Things, alas, did not work out that way, and two days later the Aussies fairly slammed us 31-6 in a match that, from a British point of view, must have evoked a good many wry memories of the famous 'Battle of Rorke's Drift' in which, over forty years ago, a British team reduced to ten men by injuries defeated the full might of Australia. Unhappily for us history did not repeat itself, but injuries were certainly unkind to us during the course of this vital World Cup match, and when it was all over our dressing-room indeed resembled a casualty station, with Alan Prescott, Tom Harris, Syd Little, Jack Grundy, and Derek Turner all needing some very real attention.

In fact, as Phil King of the *People* remarked at the time, 'Great Britain's five-man pack looked like the front end of a tram smash.' Still the 'Diggers' had been full value for their victory, and they went on to defeat France to win the Cup entirely on their merits. Possibly the drubbing we had received, in more senses than one, at the hands of the Australians had shattered the remnants of our confidence, for we turned in an absolute rank display in the final match of the series against New Zealand and were defeated 21-29. Thus ended - and in complete disaster - a series that, from our point of view, had promised so much at the start.

In more senses than one this had not been a happy venture, although from the financial angle some of the 'broke and destitute' stories that circulated back in the North of England at the time were stretching it a bit. I'll say straightaway that as a tour this was not a particularly remunerative one as far as the players and their families were concerned, but leaving authority out of it, the majority of the party had been handsomely endowed financially thanks to the kindness of their supporters' clubs back home. Jeff Stevenson and I, for example, received £150 each from the Headingley supporters' club before setting out - a truly magnificent gesture and one which was much appreciated. Although hospitality is always lavish on any Rugby League tour, a player likes to be able to return a little himself sometimes. For me, too, the tour, as I've previously described, was to have an unhappy sequel, in that my alleged conduct during the World Cup series was to cost me, or at least appeared to have cost me a third trip to Australia under League auspices.

Setbacks And Disappointments

Nevertheless, despite the friction it may have caused, this World Cup venture supplied us with an experience that seldom comes the way of any sportsman, for with the Cup series completed we travelled on to New Zealand where we played a couple of exhibitions against France, and then on to South Africa where we played two more similar matches, first of all at Benoni in the Transvaal, under the auspices of the Transvaal National Sporting Club, and then at the Jan Smuts Ground, East London.

Travel in this fabulous country was an unforgettable experience, although from a rugby football point of view I doubt whether the Rugby League will ever make a successful invasion of the country. Indeed, as is the case in my own South Wales, the South Africans are understandably conservative in their attitude towards rugby football; understandably, for they, like the Welsh, have a great tradition in Rugby Union and they are reluctant to depart from it in any shape or form.

In fact the only leading South African authority who expressed himself as favourably disposed to the thirteen-aside game was the famous Springbok rugby player and Test cricketer, Tony Harries. To me it seemed that the majority of Union critics in South Africa had already condemned Rugby League without taking the trouble to come and watch it. Perhaps that is understandable, for I am certain you cannot propagate Rugby League on merely a couple of exhibition matches - however spectacular. On the contrary, as I discovered for myself, the game grows on you as part of a gradual process. The fact that Rugby League has ousted Rugby Union as the most popular game in the North of England is not due to advertising propaganda, but rather because its followers have grown up with the game from its earliest beginnings.

RUGBY LEAGUE *v.* RUGBY UNION

After I had been at Leeds for a short time family business took me back temporarily to South Wales. While there I bumped into a prominent member of the Welsh Rugby Union at the luncheon table of a Cardiff hotel.

No, he did not cut me dead as a 'rugby renegade'. On the contrary he was friendliness itself, and seemingly very interested to learn how they conducted things up North. We chatted for quite a while, and then suddenly his features took on a half-regretful, half-reproachful look as he turned to me and said 'Ah, but Lewis, you've lost your freedom, haven't you?' I turned to hide the grin on my face, and having murmured something to the effect that 'it wasn't as bad as all that', took my leave of a gentleman whom I realized was - however misguidedly - genuinely sorry for me.

There are, I dare say, still many of my friends in South Wales who feel the same way, so here and now let me say that from a social point of view I have not found the slightest difference playing for Leeds as a professional or, say, the Barbarians as an amateur. Indeed if there is any difference at all it is that I have considerably widened the circle of my friends and social contacts as the direct result of my turning professional.

In another chapter I mentioned that in my teens I imagined the Rugby League peopled entirely by thugs and mercenaries - a point of view that I'm afraid is still foolishly subscribed to by a number of people within the Rugby Union game. I have also told how a meeting with the Leeds team manager, Mr Ken Dalby, at the Lord's Cricket Ground helped to eradicate this silly notion for me, and I can assure you that there are any number of Ken Dalbys in the League, none perhaps that I personally hold in such high esteem, educated and personable personalities with a deep sense of responsibility for both the clubs they serve and the welfare of the men who play for them and, what's more, imbued with as deep and selfless a love for the game of rugby football as you'll find anywhere.

What my Rugby Union friend really meant by his reference to my 'losing my freedom' was, I take it, the discipline and restrictions which are supposedly placed on all those who play professional sport for a living.

Now naturally the Leeds club - or for that matter any club worthy of the name - would soon have me on the mat were they to establish that I spent every evening carousing until the small hours of the morning and they would, too, most certainly object were I to neglect my training or otherwise fail to take my profession seriously, but believe me, Leeds, and to my knowledge the majority of the League clubs, gladly leave such things to the good sense of the players.

Certainly there is no snooping into one's private affairs, and if a player, especially a single chap in digs, does tend to be a bit lax or wayward in these matters, a friendly word from the coach or skipper is, you can take it from me, the serious outcome of an initial offence against the club code. I will grant that 'the anonymous letter' is part and parcel - I might say, one of the burdens - of a professional career. You will know the kind of thing I mean. You are see out at a party by some fanatical club supporter who assumes the worst and writes in to the club directorate accordingly.

I recall once during my early days at Leeds calling with my wife at a road-house outside the city where we partook of a little refreshment - in my case a fruit cordial. Leaving the hotel I tripped over a badly adjusted mat in the *foyer* and almost fell. I forgot all about the incident until I reported for training two days later when, much to my amazement, Mr Dalby chipped me, though, I suspect, half seriously, about 'staggering out drunk from a certain road-house a couple of evenings previously'.

I haven't had a similar experience since, but that I'm sure is not for the lack of correspondents - on the contrary it's just that I've been at Leeds long enough for the club officials to get to know me thoroughly and accordingly consign all such correspondence to its rightful place. Let me assure readers that the predominant feature of club-player relations at Headingley is mutual confidence, respect, and loyalty, and it is this latter quality and the great team spirit it promotes that makes the Leeds dressing-room the happy place it is.

The mention of 'team spirit' where professional rugby is concerned puts me in mind of a newspaper article I read on this very subject quite some time before I'd actually turned pro myself. The writer, a former Welsh international who, incidentally, had never played Rugby League himself, stated that the thing he disliked most about League football was 'the clocking on and off' attitude inevitably adopted by those who were engaged in the business - meaning, of course, that the League player regards the whole game merely as a job of work and that in consequence he enjoys none of the social intercourse with his 'workmates' that is such a lauded feature of Rugby Union.

I wish I could take the writer behind the scenes at Headingley for, to begin with, he would find our dressing-room no different from any Rugby Union dressing-room - he would hear the same banter, feel the same atmosphere of easy camaraderie, and altogether be disabused of the notion that professional players are grim tight-lipped individuals who think only of the pay packet. In the tea-room afterwards, too, he would quickly discover that the professional players and their wives and girl friends intermingle just as freely and as pleasantly as they do in the most exclusive amateur clubs.

In fact, I would go as far as to say that social relations in Rugby League extend rather more widely than they do in Union. Certainly they are not confined to match days or training nights, for with most of us settled down and married, the whole thing becomes very much the family circle, with everyone being more or less on visiting terms with everyone else.

What a wonderful time the wives and sweethearts of the Leeds players had over the week-end we defeated Barrow in the Challenge Cup Final at Wembley, for example, a week-end in London entirely at the expense of the Leeds club. I could not help contrasting this professional consideration and generosity with the often niggardly outlook that is evident in Rugby Union.

When I was playing in internationals in Wales it used to take me all my time fixing my family up with tickets to see the match, much less introduce them to the social side of our activities. Do not imagine I am moaning over that, for no organization, whether amateur or professional, can be expected to defray the expenses of the friends and relations of players at every match they are engaged in. Even so, we used to exchange some pretty wry glances amongst each other when at 'away' internationals in which Wales were engaged we used to grumble about the people who appeared to be able to obtain free tickets.

I recall how bitter some of us were in Dublin on the occasion of the Triple Crown 'decider' in 1952 when Len Blythe, whom injury had deprived of his place in the XV, came over to Ireland at his own expense, and stood on the bank to cheer the lads on to victory. Seeing that Len had played in the three previous internationals, and that Wales had only played eighteen players throughout the campaign, it would have imposed no burden on the finances had arrangements been made for him to be taken across with the official party.

Getting back to Rugby League, I have never regretted one moment of my time at Headingley, for travel where you wish, you could never find a finer bunch of fellows. Believe me, the Leeds team spirit, forged out of personal friendships, has got the side out of many a tight corner when mere technical efficiency has failed. I hope, therefore, that I have made it clear that I at least, and from the strictly social viewpoint, have found Rugby League not the least bit less enjoyable than Rugby Union.

What of the game itself? Is it harder to play, is it tougher, or does it require more intensive preparation and training than the Union game? My answer in every case is in the affirmative.

Since training is the essential prelude to any kind of games-playing I will discuss that first. Let me correct the rather widespread belief that Rugby League players train oftener that do their Union counterparts; on the contrary, most League players have jobs outside football which means that, like the amateurs, they have to do their training in the evenings. Just as the first-class players of clubs in Wales train on Tuesday and Thursday evenings, so do the Leeds team. There, however, the similarity ends, for Rugby League training is much more intensive and certainly more intelligently applied than are the training methods one normally encounters in Rugby Union.

The accent in Rugby League is, one might expect, emphatically upon *speed*, and by that I mean not so much the ability to run a hundred yards in evens or less as the ability to accelerate from a standing start. Indeed, since the marking and tackling in the professional game is positively razor keen, quickness off the mark becomes a vital asset, and to achieve it we spend much of our training time sprinting. This is not to say that a training session consists only of practising with starting-blocks or the rest of the athletic paraphernalia; on the contrary we merely do the obvious; i.e. repeatedly break into a flat-out sprint at the drop of the trainer's handkerchief, from either a standing or jog-trotting position. Twenty-five yards is about the maximum distance we sprint at full speed, and I can assure you this procedure, repeated half a dozen times at every training session, puts a fine edge upon your reactions, both mental and physical.

Touch rugby is another favourite on training nights up North and this, too, sharpens one's reactions enormously, besides giving the players practise with the ball. Naturally ball practise (queer that the fact is so often overlooked) figures largely in Rugby League training methods, and though it may be on occasions mentally boring to practise the same 'scissors' movement over and over again, it certainly pays dividends on match days.

Remember that the all important thing is not to master the subtleties of any move on a rugger field but to be word perfect in the execution of the fundamentals. A player might possess the 'know how' of this move or that one, but it will not help him in the least if he drops the vital pass at the crucial moment of a match. Practice, they say, makes perfect, and never was a truer word spoken when it is related to a combined movement on a rugger field. For example, I can now take Jeff Stevenson's famous back-flip blindfold nine times out of ten - not because I am an extraordinarily gifted handler but for the simple reason that I've practised with him so frequently that the whole thing becomes almost second nature.

As I stated earlier, I am dubious about the value of coaching as applied to the individual, but team coaching in the hands of an expert is quite a different kettle of fish. That is another vital difference between League and Union. In the latter game a coach tends to look for and correct faults in the individual player, but the professional coach looks at the question from a comprehensive team angle - not only his own team, but the opposition's as well. That is why your average Rugby League coach is usually able to plan his own team's strategy with an exact appreciation of the opposition's strengths and weaknesses.

Speaking exclusively from a Leeds angle, some of the team talks we receive on training nights are as penetrative and revealing as a tip-top military briefing, and many times they have enabled us to 'pull one out of the bag' when the opposition are least expecting it. No detail is, in fact, too minute for your top-class Rugby League coach to ignore, and as an instance I'll quote an incident that happened during the course of our Challenge Cup Final with Barrow at Wembley - not a particularly vital one, I'll admit, but one which nevertheless illustrates the shrewdness and real football acumen of our coach and team manager, Ken Dalby.

Before going out on to the Stadium Ken told us, 'Don't

forget these fellows will be as nervous as you are, so if you can kid them that you are confident then you're half-way there.' One of the methods by which Ken suggested we might achieve this very desirable end was to give the Barrow players the impression that we had everything all planned out to the last detail. Thus as Phil Jackson (I believe it was) came slicing through the middle early on I shouted to Keith McLellan, 'Righto, Keith, I'll take him,' whereupon Phil flashed out a pass, evidently convinced that he was covered by two Leeds players. As I say, it was not vital but it does, I suggest, illustrate the thoroughness of the professional approach to rugby.

Naturally I can imagine my Rugby Union friends wondering whether such thoroughness is necessary in their own game, which they claim is played mainly for enjoyment. The real point is, of course, that any game which is worth playing is worth playing well.

Indeed, from my own experience, and I'm sure it is a common one, I played just as hard and keenly for Llanelly and Wales as an amateur as I have done subsequently for Leeds and Great Britain as a professional. In fact, although I do not agree with many of the fabulous theories of Dr Danie Craven of South Africa on rugby football, I do most wholeheartedly applaud him for his efforts to ensure that all teams which come under his jurisdiction are trained to the hair - both technically and physically. Winning is not the be-all and end-all of playing any game, but unless your sights are set firmly on winning, there is little point in entering the lists in the first place. To me, any other attitude is just like picking up a gun at a rifle range and aiming at anything but the target.

I am asked from time to time whether I do any goal-kicking practice at training sessions. Quite candidly, apart from early season, I do not, for I believe - along with South

King of Rugger

Africa's 'Ockey' Geffin - that to kick them in practice is in most cases to miss them in matches. A great deal of nonsense is both spoken and written on the subject of goal-kicking. It is not the *exact science* it is so often cracked up to be amongst the so-called aces. Naturally I hope to score a 'bull' every time I try for the posts, but for every kick I attempt from a range greater than thirty-five yards on either side of the posts, for from such a distance it is almost impossible to have full control of a kick. What is really the difference between a kick that sails a hairsbreadth inside the posts and one that grazes its outside circumference? Three points, you will answer, and you are right, but only numerically, for as a technical achievement they are identical.

Talking of kicking, it is interesting to record that only in this aspect has Rugby League football been detrimental to my play, for as the seasons progress so does the range of my kicking diminish. My own theory is that my kicking muscle has weakened through lack of constant use, as I now obviously do not do anything like the amount of punting I used to do at Rugby Union. Mind you, I'd rather run with the ball than boot it, and you can't have it both ways - not all through life anyway.

Now to the game proper. It is my firm conviction that Rugby League is more scientific and harder to play than the Union game. At the start I found the tempo as trying on the reflexes as on my physical endurance, but once brought to concert pitch by Rugby League training methods I was able to enjoy the matches as a footballer pure and simple. There is obviously much more open play, with the result that any back worth his salt has unlimited opportunities to shine.

In my view the most difficult positions in professional rugby for the new arrival from Rugby Union are those of full-back, stand-off half and hooker. The problems facing a full-back are too obvious to need elucidating, whilst the newly signed 'hooker' has quite naturally to adapt himself to an entirely different technique in scrummaging which calls for more real skill and swiftness on the actual 'strike' than is normally needed in the Union game, where hooking is oftentimes a very devious craft indeed. It is, however, the stand-off half who is affected most by the transition. To begin with he must stand much nearer to and at a rather shallower angle from the scrum than he is obliged to as an amateur player. This means that he must get accustomed to the very swift short pass and to the need for lightning acceleration from what is practically a standing start in most cases. Another problem is that - unlike Rugby Union where the loose forward does it for him - he must at all times get up to engage his man and bring him to earth. Yes, stand-off half is a difficult position to play in Rugby League, for if nothing else it is perpetual motion both in attack and defence.

Finally the most vexed question of all. Does the fact that there are pay packets involved inevitably provoke dirty play in professional rugby? I say *no*. Although rugby under any code of laws is not a game renowned for gentleness, there is in Rugby League a pretty strong deterrent to those who would seek to win by questionable tactics; i.e. marching orders from the referee, followed by suspension by the League's Disciplinary Committee and, in consequence, the loss of a weekly wage packet for a stipulated period. Thus the pay packet, which in the eyes of many is the cause of dirty play, becomes in actual practice the greatest safeguard against it.

I'll grant that there are players who still get out of hand occasionally, but let's face it - so too are there many such in Rugby Union. In both games, however, we can be perfectly sure that they are outnumbered by those who play within the spirit as well as the letter of the laws.

20

RUGBY UNION'S BEST

As a schoolboy during the war years I remember being taken to watch one of the Service internationals staged on the St. Helens ground at Swansea and, allowing for the impressionability of youth, I still swear that the rugby football played that afternoon was the greatest I have ever seen.

I am not alone in the belief, for many veteran followers of the game in South Wales have since told me that the rugby produced by the League and Union stars who played alongside each other in these wartime matches was a replica of the stuff Trew, Owen, Bancroft, and the rest used to produce on this same famous ground way back in the 'Golden Era' of the game in Wales.

No wonder. Alongside and in opposition to each other in the Service internationals were such players as Gus Risman, Haydn Tanner, Willy Davies, Alun Edwards, Ernest Ward, Roy Francis, Jackie Lawrenson, and Bleddyn Williams, and if their presence on any one football field was not calculated to spellbind an audience then nothing will ever be.

The memory of these wartime matches inevitably lingers on, and it is almost certain that a major proportion of the rugby spectators would indeed welcome an annual trial of strength in the shape of a Test match between two sides labelled Rugby League and Rugby Union. It is equally certain that any such contest would produce rugby football just as thrilling and memorable as the Service internationals. Unfortunately - failing the outbreak of another world war which no one in any case wants - Rugby Union *versus* Rugby League will for ever remain the pipe-dream of the true enthusiast, for the prospects of it ever becoming a reality are remoter these days than at perhaps any time in history.

Dream or reality, however, supporters of both codes will continue to while away many a leisure hour at the time-honoured pastime of team-picking for such an event. I therefore need little excuse to join them, with the added advantage that I have played both codes and am accordingly eligible, if not eminently so, to sit on both selection committees. I'll start then by choosing from the players I have actually played against the fifteen I consider most worthy to represent the *world* at Rugby Union. I'm assuming of course each of my selections to be at peak form at the time of selection.

To begin with the choice is easy where the full-back position is concerned - it is not so much a matter of choice as necessity - for Bob Scott of New Zealand is surely a 'must'. And unless it be Johnny Buchler of South Africa, I cannot think of an adequate reserve for Scott, much less a serious rival. Yes, Bob Scott was far and away the greatest full-back I encountered in Rugby Union despite the fact that his greatest days were behind him when we played against each other at Eden Park in 1950. I'll grant that it didn't look much like it three years later when he was the star of the New Zealand tour in this country.

Next on the list are the wing three-quarters, and for me it's Ken Jones (Wales) on the right and J.K.'Chum' Osche of South Africa on the left. It has been by no means an easy choice, for J.V.Smith of England and Pomathios of France were two cracking good wings I played both with and against during the period. I have seen Smith score several tries that were quite out of this world for sheer individual brilliance. Individual ability apart, however, the thing that always impressed me about Osche and Ken Jones was the absolute certainty with which they capitalized on any reasonable opportunity of scoring.

Believe me, it adds tremendously to the morale and confidence of any back division to know that out on the flanks they have a couple of players capable of turning to account the least semblance of a scoring chance. Added to their certainty in this direction, both Jones and Osche were fast and intelligent players who could defend as well as attack, and neither were 'injury prone' - as is so often the case with the real 'fliers' of rugby football. Some people will doubtless agree that the massive Wasps player was a handy man to have in any side but, with due deference to the power of those tank-like burst of his, Ted cut very little ice with an opponent who got quickly into him before he'd attained full momentum.

At centre my choices are those of my fellow Welshmen, Bleddyn Williams and Jackie Matthews. Formidable at any time, they were of undoubted world class during the tour of New Zealand and Australia and were just about the perfect foil for each other - Bleddyn with his classical technique and baffling sidestep, and Jackie with his straight, thrustful running and devastating tackling.. Bleddyn, too, was no laggard when it came to tackling. If his methods were not as spectacular as his partner, it was no joke encountering his broad shoulder with the impetus of something like thirteen stone plus behind it.

Naturally I realize that there are several other contenders for these positions, for both Clive van Rynveld and Louis Cannell of England were in the absolute top bracket as attacking centres, whilst Trevor Allen (Australia) and Ryk van Schoor (South Africa) were almost in the Matthews class as destroyers of the opposing mid-field attack, but for all-round brilliance no pair I ever played with or against in Rugby Union matched up to the Cardiff pair.

As far as the outside-half position is concerned there is again no dearth of candidates. Among my contemporaries in Rugby Union were Jack Kyle (Ireland), Billy Cleaver and Cliff Morgan (Wales), Martin Regan and Ivor Preece (England), and Hannes Brewis (South Africa) - all in their different ways truly magnificent players.

Four of them - Kyle, Brewis, Preece, and Cleaver - might be described as real expert tacticians in the modern manner, while Regan and Cliff Morgan (leastways when I played with him) veered more towards the traditional in the way of creating openings for their centres by elusive running and breaking. Kyle was, to my mind, the only one who could alternate perfectly between the modern and the classical, for while his genius as an attacking outside half was given full reign in New Zealand and Australia, he also proved over and again with Ireland that he could play to perfection the tactical role demanded of an outside half in modern Triple Crown rugby. Indeed, it was Jack Kyle - aided and abetted by the Irish pack - who laid down the formula for this type of rugby and I am quite certain that if Ireland had possessed mid-field backs to match his own outstanding ability, then Jackie could just as easily have switched to the all-out attacking game that so thrilled the crowds 'Down

King of Rugger

Under'. As a stand-off half, I am convinced Jackie had all it takes - lightning acceleration off the mark, a fine pair of hands, elusiveness, judgement, a fine kick and, not the least, a fighting heart to match his wonderful ability. He is a 'must' for any world fifteen I pick.

The choosing of a partner for Kyle is not such an easy business, because in my view the standard of scrum-half play has not been particularly high over the period I played in international Rugby Union. In fact, physical strength and a long pass seemed attributes far more sought after than genuine footballing ability, with the result that your international scrum half conformed strictly to a type. O'Meara, Kyle's Irish partner, A.W Black (Scotland), Gordon Rimmer (England), and Rex Willis of Wales were all solid, if unimaginative, players, and from a Home point of view I think Rex Willis was the best of the bunch for he possessed a beautifully streamlined service from the scrum and with it all the guts in the world to withstand the batterings of the back-row forwards. Even so I consider the best I encountered during the period was the South African, P.A. 'Fonny' du Toit, who had all the attributes the others had plus a real old-soldier type of cunning around the field generally. He was, too, a clever kicker both on the open and blind side of the scrum, and often used his ability in this direction to switch the direction of attack when the opposition were least expecting it.

Back-row forwards of true world class are, of course, two a penny, which means that I personally would be perfectly happy with any three out of a dozen candidates. Certainly I would not relish the task of any professional selector who had to discriminate between the claims of such players as Hennie Muller, Basie van Wyk (South Africa), Pat Crowley (New Zealand), Bill Mackay and Jim McCarthy (Ireland), Doug Elliott (Scotland), Des O'Brien (Ireland), John

Gwilliam, Bob Evans, Ray Cale and Clem Thomas (Wales), and Vic Roberts (England), for all of them were players of the highest class in their own specialized positions. Discrimination, however there has to be, for 'pins', I take it, are taboo even on private selection committees.

Thus my back row would read: Ray Cale (blind side), Hennie Muller (lock), and Doug Elliott (open side). Muller was one of the most complete footballers I ever saw in the back row of any scrum. He always seemed in perfect command of every situation, possessed an ice-cool football brain, and his great speed enabled him to make some incredible interventions as a coverer behind his own backs. Cale, of course - on the form he showed for Wales in the Triple Crown season of 1950 - was undoubtedly the greatest blind-side wing-forward in the world, and as a destroyer of the opponent's attack I have never seen anyone quite like him. His tackling was bone-crunching stuff, as opponents will testify, but I think the secret of his proficiency as a spoiler lay in his wonderful sense of balance and timing - qualities that ensured he was seldom caught on the wrong foot by even the most elusive of opponents. You will remember that I said my world fifteen is being selected on the basis of peak form. This is precisely why I include Doug Elliott of Scotland as my open-side wing-forward in preference to other players of perhaps wider renown. Believe me - or if you don't, then ask the members of the Welsh fifteens which played at Murrayfield in 1949 and 1951 - Elliott in peak form was a force to reckon with. Indeed, on his best days he was something that few outside halves could cope with. Fast, strong, an engulfing tackler, and quite ruthless in his method and outlook, Douglas Elliott is certainly my choice. Mind you, I wish I could cap it with the proviso that the match was to be played at Murrayfield, for it was there he was apt to play his greatest.

Needless to say that the great line-out jumper, Roy John

of Wales, must come into the reckoning for a place in any world fifteen, but with all other things being equal I consider physique should be the determining factor here. It is true Roy was possibly the greatest line-out specialist playing international rugby between 1950-2, but not so very far behind him in this aspect of the game were people like J. ('Salty') du Rand of South Africa and R.A. ('Snow') White of New Zealand, both of them magnificent scrummagers and rather more powerful and rugged in their general play than was Roy, even at his peak and for all his great skill. Du Rand and White, then, are my second row. It is with regret that I have to bypass such herculean characters as Rhys Stephens, Don Hayward (Wales), and J.D. Nelson (Ireland).

Finally the front row. Chris Koch of South Africa strikes me as the most automatic choice of them all, for this squatly built Springbok prop was power personified. To challenge for the other front-row positions there are any number of truly great scrummaging forwards - Cliff Davies, Billy Williams, Don Hayward (Wales), Tom Clifford (Ireland), R..V.Stirling (England), Don Budge (Scotland), Kevin Skinner (New Zealand), to mention but a few of them.

If you are prepared to look for your men outside the international arena there was my Gorseinon 'townie', Douglas Jones, who over ten seasons with Swansea proved himself one of the toughest of them all. During his career with Swansea Doug Jones played against the touring teams of all three major rugby countries: New Zealand, South Africa, and Australia. I am told that in every case his opponents expressed complete mystification over his non-selection for Wales. As in the second row, however, power and physique weight heavily in my consideration, with the result that I can think of no finer support for Chris Koch than that likely to be provided by the New Zealander, Kevin Skinner - a real rugged type, this one.

For the hooking berth, my vote goes instantly to Karl

Mullen of Ireland. Apart from being an expert on the strike, he is well worth his place in any international fifteen for his ability as an all-round forward. My final selection would thus read:

R.W.H. Scott (New Zealand); K.J. Jones (Wales), Jack Matthews (Wales), Bleddyn Williams (Wales), J.K.Osche (South Africa); J.W. Kyle (Ireland), P.A. du Toit (South Africa); C. Koch (South Africa), K.D. Mullen (Ireland), K. Skinner (New Zealand), J. du Rand (South Africa), R.A. White (New Zealand), W.R. Cale (Wales), Hennie Muller (South Africa), W.I.D. Elliott (Scotland).

I would make South Africa's Muller skipper, for though Bleddyn Williams and Karl Mullen would be both shrewd-enough tacticians to undertake the job I make no secret of my admiration for the tough uncompromising South African approach to Test rugby. Hennie Muller, to my mind, typified this approach, and would be the ideal man to lead the Rugby Union into action against the pick of the Rugby League.

For me, then, it's now a quick skip across the fence to choose a Rugby League representative side to try conclusions with the formidable team I've just chosen. I can't help thinking that many 'professional' selectors must envy me my freedom of movement in these matters!

21

RUGBY LEAGUE'S BEST

Picking the world's best Rugby League team is, for obvious reasons, a far harder and more discriminating task than the sorting out of the *corp d'elite* of Rugby Union.

If any of my Rugby Union readers would question this assertion on the grounds that the Union game is played on a far wider basis than League, then let me counter by pointing out that in the course of say two seasons (the normal interval between League tours) more players enter and depart from the international scene than is the case in Rugby Union.

The reason for this is that owing to the fierce tempo of the professional game a player's international career in the League game is shorter. This means that where players of international calibre are concerned the field of selection is far wider. Then again, in professional rugby the gap between the average club player and the international is far narrower than it is in the Union game, with the result that you could in most instances cover each representative team you picked with a 'shadow' team of almost the same standard. Indeed, before I pick a single player of my world selection to oppose the Rugby Union stars I've already picked I realize full well that I am about to make myself a wide-open target for almost every fan and critic in the business.

Still, I've had my share of the 'bird' before so with the same provisos - that every player is assumed to be at peak form, and that I've considered no player whose career has not run parallel with my own - down to business. Let me add that I'm making this 'test' a fifteen-aside affair under Rugby Union rules. That at least will enable me to include a couple of fine forwards who would otherwise have had to be omitted.

First, then, full-back. Who right away would volunteer to make the final selection from a field that includes Clive Churchill (Australia), Puig Albert (France), Johnny Hunter (Huddersfield), Bert Cook (Leeds), Jack Cuncliffe (Wigan), Gus Risman (Workington), Fred Miller (Featherstone), Ted Cahill (Rochdale), Glyn Moses (St Helens), Andre Rives (France), and Jimmy Ledgard (Leigh) I don't relish the task, but it has got to be done and I'll plump for the Australian maestro Clive Churchill.

Ideally, I suppose, the full-back should be the team's place-kicker, in which respect there are perhaps surer feet than Clive's in the business. Yet from a purely League angle - which regards attack and defence as complementary attributes) I should say that the Australian in peak form was just about the best all-rounder of the lot. I've a sneaking feeling, though, that had Gus Risman played out his entire career as a full-back he might easily have been one of the all-time greats. He was past the autumn of his career when I played against him, yet his skill, shrewdness, and complete poise stamped him as a master.

In the case of wing three-quarters the Union can never possibly hold a candle to the professional game - and this is chiefly, I suppose, because the Rugby League game really uses its speed merchants in preference to turning them into wing-forwards or else delegating them with a merely ornamental role. Indeed, when I was selecting my Rugby Union side I could only think of three really outstanding wings I had played with or against during my career as an amateur - Ken Jones, J.K.Osche, and J.V. Smith. Now contrast that with the position in Rugby League, where I can take my pick from a whole galaxy of wonderful wings including Brian Bevan (Warrington), Billy Boston (Wigan), Mike Sullivan (Wigan), Lionel Cooper, Peter Henderson (Huddersfield), Drew Turnbull (Leeds), Harper Daniels (Halifax), Jim Lewthwaite (Barrow), Kerel von Vollehoven [sic] (St Helens), Jackie Lawrenson (Workington), Terry O'Grady (Oldham) - not forgetting the famous 'Bison of Valcluse', Savonne of France - and you will perhaps appreciate the enormity of the task I have set myself.

Fortunately there is one 'must' in any sport you care to mention - Bradman in cricket, Stan Matthews in association football - and by the same token Brian Bevan in the Rugby League game. This slightly balding, not too robustly built Australian is without a doubt one of the greatest wing-men the game has ever seen. Speed and pure footballing ability apart, he was an absolute past master at the art of concealing his pace. Time and again opponents, myself amongst them, could have sworn that the Warrington flier was going full bat, only to find him producing a last-second surge of pace to leave them and the spectators breathless. Unfortunately I never saw that other great Australian, Eric Harris, play for Leeds, but if he had anything on Brian Bevan in the matter of working variations on the theme of pace then he must have been a marvel indeed.

On the assumption that wings, like centre three-quarters, operate best when their individual abilities are so widely separated as to make them foils for each other I was tempted in the first place to include Brian's countryman, the powerful high-striding Huddersfield wing, Lionel Cooper, on the opposite flank, but on second thoughts I'm pretty sure that, on peak form, my own countryman, Billy Boston, concedes little to Cooper in the way of thrusting, running, and hard tackling. I'm quite certain that as an all-round footballer the Wigan wing is far the superior.

Centre three-quarters - and I mean cracking good ones - are sure plentiful in the Rugby League and accordingly the choice problem is not so much as who to put in but who to leave out. In my own times I have played with and against centres who would hold their own in any company - stylists like Ernie Ashcroft of Wigan, Phil Jackson of Barrow, the incomparable Ernest Ward of Bradford, New Zealand's Lynch of Halifax, strong thrusters in the persons of the Australian quartet Harry Wells, Alec Watson, Keith McLellan, Tony Paskins (Workington), and last-ditch defenders such as Trevor Allen (Leigh) and Doug Greenall (St Helens). For my money, however, it's Ernie Ashcroft of Wigan paired alongside that fine all-round footballer from Barrow, Phil Jackson. I fancy they would supply any defence with more problems than they could cope with.

At stand-off half - with due deference to the great achievements of such as Ray Price (Warrington), Dickie Williams (Leeds), and Cec Mountford (Wigan) - I think I should be inclined to bank on the guile and matchless experience of Barrow's Billy Horne. There are few players, either in League or Union, who can dictate the course of a match in quite the same manner as this great Barrow footballer at his best. Billy Horne had his greatest days well behind him when he played for Barrow against us in the 1957 Cup Final, but his tactical generalship was even then of the very highest and throughout that exciting second half we always had the feeling, one might almost describe it as a dread, that if anyone was going to steal the match from us, it would be the Barrow captain and stand-off half.

When in Australia in 1954 I saw Gerry Helme of Warrington pitted against Australia's great scrum half, Keith Holman, and in their contrasting styles they were undoubtedly two of the world's best at the period, but even in my own brief span the Rugby League has contained any number of brilliant scrum hales. I think of men like Jim Haig of New Zealand - a strong, shrewd, and vastly experienced player - my own countryman, Billy Banks of Huddersfield, Tommy Bradshaw of Wigan, and several others. However, probably because I've had occasion to admire his genius so often and at such close quarters, my choice is my own club mate, Jeff Stevenson of Leeds - one of the greatest natural footballers playing in Rugby League today.

Where the forwards are concerned I'm almost tempted, in fact I am tempted, to use a pin or else draw them out of a hat. Certainly I don't feel qualified to discriminate between the claims of the score or more of world-class forwards I've played with and against during my half-dozen seasons as a professional. For what my views are worth, however, here on a Rugby Union basis are eight forwards I'd welcome (I won't say *prefer*) in my World Rugby League Fifteen:

Front row: Alan Prescott (St Helens), Ken Kearney (Australia), Nat Silcock (Wigan). *Second row*: Jack Grundy (Barrow), Arthur Clues (Australia). *Back row*: Davy Valentine (Huddersfield), Ike Owen (Leeds), Ken Traill (Bradford).

Thus my completed team would read:

Clive Churchill; Brian Bevan, Ernie Ashcroft, Phil Jackson, Billy Boston; Billy Horne, Jeff Stevenson; Alan Prescott (captain), Ken

Kearney, Nat Silcock, Jack Grundy, Arthur Clues, Davy Valentine, Ike Owen, Ken Traill.

Who would win this battle of the giants? For my money it would be the Rugby League side, though matters would no doubt be desperately even for most of the game. There would come a point, I believe, midway through the second half when pace and fitness would sway the issue in favour of the professionals. I might be wrong, but that 's the way I see it. Whatever the result, one thing is certain - this would be a match to live long in the memory.

Naturally, both modesty and my 'neutrality' as a selector precludes me from a place in either of these sides, but needless to say I would dearly like to participate in a match of this description, preferably as a centre three-quarter.

Indeed, that might serve to answer for all time the question that is most frequently asked of me where rugby football is concerned - which position do you like playing best? It is, in fact, centre three-quarter, for although I have on occasions and with a fair measure of success played at full-back, wing three-quarter and at stand-off half in international rugby, I like centre, and I believe that it is the position which best suits my style of play.

22

ATTACK IS THE KEY WORD

Not so long ago an attack of bronchitis having given me one of my rare Saturdays before my own fireside, I was able to 'look in' on my first Rugby Union international game for several years. The match televised was the England-Scotland match at Murrayfield and, in the mode of so many of the post-war internationals, it was not particularly attractive to watch.

As is so often the case the forwards were mainly in charge with the backs but rarely in action, and only then with stereotyped passing movements which invariably ended with the wing-man being crowded into touch. Then quite out of the blue the England centres, Butterfield and Phillips, worked a perfect 'scissors' movement - so sudden and perfect in fact that it seemed to illuminate the whole game with the vividness of forked lightning in a winter sky.

Coming as it did out of a background of mediocre and ineffectual play, this one single flash of authentic skill not only etched itself on the memory but seemed also to offer full compensation for much of the dreary stuff that had gone before. I am not advocating, of course, that rugby's most skillful movements should be rationed to one or two per match, but I do think that oftentimes - in Rugby League particularly - we tend to over-elaborate to an extent that makes the spectators *blasé*, if not actually bored, with sleight-of-hand passing and similar refinements.

I do most seriously suggest that we work to death the 'scissors' movement and the reverse pass in Rugby League football, not only to the spectators' detriment but the players as well. Undoubtedly the frequency with which the normal professional back division attempts this kind of manoeuvre destroys almost completely the element of surprise. From a spectator's point of view a surfeit of reverse passes is quite as boring to watch as an epidemic of kicking to touch. Variety, I'm quite sure, is the spice of rugby football, both for spectators and players as well.

If I am ever given the task of passing on advice or instruction to the young up-and-coming player I shall warn them above all else of the dangers of becoming set in technique, method, or tactics. Enjoyment is the essence of rugby football, and you certainly can't enjoy your own game, much less make it enjoyable for others, if you persist in clinging rigidly to the orthodox even in situations that cry out for variety or experiment.

Time and again during the post-war period I have heard and read of the winging forward being blamed for the decline of Rugby Union football as a spectacle. While I agree that his activities restrict these of the midfield attackers, I can never agree that they stifle them altogether. On the contrary I'm convinced that the winging forward is more often than not assisted in his allotted mission by the lack of imagination - one might almost term it 'conservatism' - of modern back play. Why, for instance, must the scrum half, on nine occasions out of every ten, pass the ball religiously to his heavily marked partner? Why must the stand-off and centres always stand in the positions dictated by custom? And why, oh why, should it be regarded as almost sinful to attack from one's one goalposts?

I am quite convinced that the answer to any rugby strategy, whether ancient or modern, is variety and unexpectedness of method, for no system of defence - however well organized and disciplined - can ever remain totally proof against opponents who constantly vary their methods. Indeed, if you can keep the opposition constantly guessing as to your intentions you are already pretty close to inducing it to panic and error. In this respect I can well remember what an unnerving business it used to be lining up in defence in the Welsh twenty-five when Ireland, with the loose head, seemed certain to gain the possession. The name engraved on all those fluttering hearts was, I assure you (and in capital letters), JACK KYLE, for in his heyday it was practically impossible to predict exactly what this great little outside half would do with the ball when it reached him. He had us all on tenterhooks, and any player who can achieve that is more than half-way towards mastering the wing-forward menace.

You will, no doubt, have noticed that throughout this discussion on variety of method I have been concerned exclusively with attack, and I make no apology for this preoccupation.

Ever since I started playing rugby seriously at the Gowerton County School during the war years I have never deviated from the belief that the game is first and foremost an attacking game. It is a belief that I put into practice from the very first moment of any match - club or international.

As I have already told, John Gwilliam instructed me to

bang my kick-off in my first international at Twickenham as far down into English territory as I possibly could. The instruction was in my case hardly necessary, for as part of my outlook on the whole game I regard the long kick-off as the essential prelude to attacking rugby. To me, at any rate, it signifies an intention of attacking the enemy goal-line from the word go.

Generally speaking, and in Rugby Union certainly, I have little patience with the tactical short kick which aims to put the ball amongst one's own forwards. In most cases it merely serves to force you immediately on the defensive. It's always the long soaring kick for me - deep into the enemy twenty-five - and nine times out of ten you are certain to gain ground, like as not if there is a fumble or knock-on at the receiving end, a tremendous tract of it. Attack then is my aim from the moment I set foot on a rugby field, and I endeavour to fulfil that aim regardless of the position I happen to be playing in.

During my Rugby Union days I used to surprise the crowds, and no doubt the opponents too, by starting attacks from my own twenty-five whilst playing in the full-back position, and even though I was more often than not successful in linking up with my colleagues in front there was always a feeling that I was exceeding my function and by doing so jeopardizing the interests of the side I was playing for. Now I cannot for the life of me understand the line of reasoning behind such a viewpoint, for I'm perfectly convinced that the primary function of every player on a rugger field - from full-back to hooker, in fact - is to help his team to cross their opponent's goal-line. And as far as I'm concerned one is far more likely to achieve this end through the elements of surprise and the unexpected.

Full-back is, I suggest, as favourable a position as any to *attack* from on a rugby field, for not only is the surprise factor in your favour but in addition your opponents are nearly always in open formation, which makes the break-through a far more likely proposition than from a scrummage or line-out when the defence is organized and prepared for most developments. Indeed, in Rugby League football the full-back position has long been regarded as one of the 'spring-boards' of attack and it often puzzles me why it should not be regarded even more so as such in Rugby Union where misdirected touch-kicks and badly aimed short punts supply the occupant of the position with a service of the ball that any stand-off half would envy.

Time and again in fact I've fielded the ball inside my own twenty-five with the nearest opponent quite fifteen yards away from me. Thus with precious seconds to spare I've had ample opportunity to study the lie of the land and act accordingly. I suggest, too, that there is nothing particularly brilliant in avoiding the tackles of on-rushing forwards, for the advantage is all with the full-back, with the result that a feint in either direction is usually enough to throw the opponents off balance and an acceleration of pace does the rest. Apart, however, from starting movements off his own bat, the full-back can become a formidable agency in attack by intervening unexpectedly in ordinary passing movements instigated by his halves and three-quarters.

Bob Scott used to do this kind of thing frequently - too frequently, I'm afraid - to produce the all-essential element of surprise. My ideal in this respect was Scott's fellow countryman, the Leeds full-back, Bert Cook, who was a past master at the art of concealing his intentions in this way. Thus, backed by the element of complete surprise and moreover by the impetus of something like thirteen and a half stone in full momentum, Bert's intrusions between his own stand-off half and centres took a terrific amount of stopping.

Attack Is The Key Word

In all rugby - professional rugby particularly - 'surprise' is the essence of attack, and if you can lend to its application the ability to vary your running pace then you have gone a very long way towards becoming a successful player. Not that this command of, or control of, pace is the special gift that a football providence reserves for the favoured few; on the contrary it can be acquired simply by establishing your maximum running speed and then ringing the changes according to the needs of a given situation to begin with. Personally I got to realize its possibilities very early in life and, as is so often the case, more or less by accident.

I first remember using the 'stop and start' technique during luncheon hour kick-abouts at the Gowerton County School - when I stopped the others did as well. While they were still hesitant, I crammed on that little extra spurt and was past them before they'd properly realized what was happening. That, with a few refinements, is the technique that has carried me fairly successfully through a few hundred rugger games of varying degrees of importance, and occasionally I can't help smiling over the fact that a schoolboy ruse has so often enabled me to steer a passage through international defences. I have, of course, been aided as always by my share of good fortune, but just the same I think there's a moral in it - in other words, when a player reaches the adult stage he is apt to over-theorize and overlook the fact that a technique or stratagem employed successfully in school or junior football can oftentimes be just as successful when employed against the tense and prestige-fraught background of an international.

Change of pace and the complementary ability to accelerate into top gear in a split second is, I am sure, the most priceless asset any footballer can command - backs above all others. The side-step, the dummy, the swerve, and occasionally sheer impetus and strength can assist you to punch a hole in the midfield defence, but none of these methods, I suggest, are as clear-cut or as unfailingly effective as a change of pace followed by a surge of real speed.

Theoretically, of course, and indeed in face of man-to-man tackling, the dummy and the drive through an opponent are easily checked, whilst the swerve and side-step, however deceptive, have a tendency to steer the line across-field towards the touchline, whereas a change of pace can, times without number, take a player past an opponent, creating in the process the illusion that his passage was actually facilitated by the opposition.

Back in Wales I was once told by a well-meaning coach that 'the difference between first and second-class rugby was that in the former class the participants went full out from the first whistle and sustained the tempo right through, whereas in second-class rugby the tendency was to play in spurts'. Now leaving aside the fact that I have actually played in second-class games in which the tempo was, to say the least, brisk from first whistle to last, I cannot agree that it is the mark of a first-class player, a back more especially, to call up every ounce of his reserves of speed and skill in every movement he takes part in.

Indeed, what applies to rugby football in this sense applies to other games as well. Do you, for example, see Ray Lindwall or Fred Trueman hurl down every ball of an over with the maximum pace at their command? Or by the same token do you see Stan Matthews or Tom Finney hare-off down the wing, like sprinters dead-set on reaching the tape every time they receive the ball? No - it's *control* which is the vital factor, the control which enables any athlete not so much as to cram on but to *possess* in the first place that little bit extra for the crucial moment.

A classic example in Rugby League is that of Warrington's great Australian wing, Brian Bevan, who time and again seems to glide effortlessly past an opponent. From the grandstand, at least, he appears to be well covered. The truth is that Brian has so perfectly modulated his running that not even his own colleagues can really detect the acceleration from cruising speed to full boost.

Throughout this chapter I have kept on referring to the 'surprise element' in rugby, and since this is a chapter written mainly for (I hope) the guidance and encouragement of those with their careers ahead I make no apology for doing so once more - this time in relation to the vexed question of' tactical kicking'.

Rugby League football, of course, soon separates the footballer from the mere booter of the ball, but in Rugby Union the modern concentration on forward play, in international matches particularly, has bred a new regime amongst backs. Many mid-field players owe their inclusion primarily to their ability to support their forwards along the touchlines and to their ability to create opportunities for their wings by means of shrewdly placed punts. I'll grant straightaway that such tactics are largely forced on modern mid-field players by the intensification of back-row spoiling methods, but I do at the same time contest most strenuously the theory that a player is worth a place in an international fifteen exclusively on the merit of being able to kick a rugby ball accurately.

Neither will I agree that such methods are the only ones open to a stand-off half or centre in modern Rugby Union. On the contrary, kicking to me is only another aspect of a multi-faceted game. Consequently, if it is overdone, then the process becomes just as futile as the business of passing for the mere sake of passing. Indeed, with kicking, as with all other aspects of the game, the all essential is *Surprise*, again with the capital 'S', and nowhere is this more strikingly emphasized than in the Rugby League where, amid an environment that is almost exclusively one of handling and passing, the sudden astutely placed 'grubber' often produces a try through the very nature of its unexpectedness.

In this respect I wonder exactly how many of the hundred and one kicks ahead, diagonal punts, and the rest that are essayed in the Union game during the course of a normal season do in fact produce a score? Judging at least from my experience as a full-back at Rugby Union, I should say not many, for in numerous matches I've simply lost count of the number of badly directed punts ahead I used to retrieve inside my own twenty-five. Not only were they badly directed, but directed also with absolutely no regard for the tactical situation. In fact some of these chaps playing at stand-off half used to make my job ridiculously easy, for all I had to do at scrum or line-out was position myself in relation to the stand-off half's kicking boot - they did the rest. The tragedy of it was, and in fact still is that in Rugby Union today any kind of kicking is looked upon as 'tactical' kicking, whereas what it so often really amounts to is kicking as the least line of resistance.

I'd go as far as to say that during my whole career in Rugby Union I only encountered four players whom I will instantly admit as true experts at this branch of the game. They were Jack Kyle (Ireland), Hannes Brewis (South Africa), Billy Cleaver, and Alun Thomas (both of Wales). All four kicked with real shrewdness, faultless accuracy, and moreover always to tactical advantage. It is significant too that all four were, in addition, top class all-round footballers, which means that kicking with them was merely the means towards a tactical end - certainly it never became the end itself. To all young players I would say: learn to kick skilfully and accurately by all means, but never to the neglect of your mastery over the techniques of running, jinking, and passing. The footballer will always outclass the robot, so don't let anyone kid you otherwise.

If I would advocate any type of kick as an especially

valuable tactical weapon for both League and Union then I would suggest the 'stab' or 'grubber' kick. Executed at top speed there is no more deadly antidote to shadow tackling. You've seen it happen many times - a centre breaks through and races up to the full-back, only to find his wing outside him policed by a couple of covering defenders. I've often observed that the centre's reaction is to essay an over-arm lob pass - which is usually knocked down by the intervening coverers. The right answer is, of course, the 'grubber', guided swiftly and in one movement through the gap for either the kicker or wing to run on to.

I'm glad to observe, though, that the 'grub kick' seems nowadays to have been adopted piecemeal by Union players. It is a far better method of countering tight marking than the lofted short punt that used to be so much a part of the Union game. The reason is obvious. A ball kicked along the ground does not have to come down and, time factor apart, can be guided much more accurately.

I've already tentatively discussed coaching in earlier chapters. I stated then that I regard team coaching as a very valuable and necessary thing indeed (although my good friends Arthur Clues and Bob McMaster would probably differ), but I am not completely convinced that, unless in the hands of a real expert, it is good for young players - not in large doses anyway.

To begin with, I am rather in agreement with Sir Leonard Hutton when he said that he was always suspicious of advice that did not come from those who had been in the middle themselves. That is not to disparage the keen non-player who endeavours to teach youngsters the rudiments of the game, but in rugby football, as in most things, theory and actual practice are two entirely different things. Only a person who has actually played the game can really measure what is important and what is not.

King of Rugger

I was, as I have said, lucky that my coach at Gowerton, Mr Bill Bowen, was an old player and therefore appreciated that results always count before method on a rugby field. Indeed, if I had been able to drop a goal from half-way with my knee-cap whilst I was under his jurisdiction I doubt whether Bill would have suggested any way I might develop my technique along more orthodox lines. On the contrary, he was content to judge a player's style by the results it brought him, and only when it was having an adverse effect on his performance was he likely to intervene with a word of advice or correction. That, as I see it, is the most valuable coaching a young player can receive, and unfortunately it is a rarer type than one might perhaps expect, for by and large the average coach seems to worry overmuch about niceties of style and technique.

Frankly, I don't think it matters a hoot which foot a player passes with provided the ball plumps straight and true and into the hands of the player for whom it was intended. I am reminded of a story I heard about a famous Yorkshire cricket coach who was bowling to a youngster at the Headingley nets, and who was becoming increasingly annoyed as his protégé walloped every delivery as hard and far as he could regardless of style or technique. Finally the young man sent a huge steepling hit to the far outfield, whereupon the coach exploded with the exclamation, 'Just look at feet,' only to hear the magnificently disdainful reply, '_____ feet, look at _____ ball.'

23

THE WAR

When the whistle blew to signify the end of that titanic Wales South Africa struggle at Cardiff Arms Park in December, 1952, I immediately stripped off my Welsh jersey and handed it in accordance with custom to my immediate opponent, Paul Johnstone, the South African right wing.

Paul was unable to give me his own jersey in return, for the Springbok fellows were restricted, it seems, to one 'swap' a tour. By the time Paul had a jersey ready for me I had turned professional, and having listened many times to the tales of chaps being ostracised by their Union pals once they had turned over to the League I confess that I had 'written off' my Springbok jersey. Imagine my surprise and delight, therefore, when one morning the postman brought me a package containing the jersey and a pleasantly worded note from the sender - Paul Johnstone.

I mention this incident as evidence to support my own firm conviction that it is seldom the players of rugby football who pursue this, to my mind, silly, futile, and wholly unnecessary vendetta between League and Union.

Let me say straight away that I not only agree with, but actually applaud, the Rugby Union's endeavours to keep their game on a purely amateur basis. Whatever views you may hold to the contrary, I feel you must acknowledge that a whole lot of people prefer to play their sport as amateurs, so why then beef at those who do their best to ensure that they are enabled to do so?

What is more, I sincerely believe that as far as the everyday conduct of the game is concerned it is far better that pros and amateurs should keep apart from each other. The reasons are of course obvious. You cannot foster loyalty and team spirit on a system that allows for only half a dozen members of a team being paid, while it is equally obvious that such a system would constitute an absolute paradise to the 'pseudo amateur'.

This objection though does not, I submit, preclude altogether the prospect of amateur and professional players from playing alongside or against each other on every occasion. No one, I'm sure, who saw those wonderful Inter-Service games during the war years will argue other than that their intermingling can produce brilliant rugby, and on that score alone I suggest that it would be a wonderful thing for rugby football were international rugby to become truly international in actual representation as well as name.

In other words when Wales play England, or France takes on Australia, the teams chosen should be fully representative of the rugby strength of the countries concerned by the inclusion of the very greatest players irrespective of whether they normally play the League or Union game. Money does not enter into this part of the argument, and I am confident that I echo the viewpoint of the majority of my fellow professionals when I say that the honour of representing one's country is one more coveted than any pay packet.

Certainly international rugby (and goodness knows it needs to) would benefit as a spectacle from the infusion of a few of the real professors of Rugby League, whilst from the player's point of view the honour of gaining an international cap would be immeasurably the greater for the knowledge that it had been gained from competition that could justly be described as truly national.

Indeed, in this respect I can tell you that there are some pretty wry glances exchanged in Rugby League dressing-rooms when we read in the newspapers that 'Butterfield and Davies' - for example - 'are the best pair of centres in the country'. By the same token, I imagine that our Rugby Union friends are often hard put to agree with the claims sometimes put forward on behalf of Rugby League players. It would settle a lot of arguments if the players of both codes were occasionally given an opportunity of putting such arguments to the test.

International matches apart, another intriguing prospect is an annual Test match between League and Union played in alternate years at Odsal Stadium and Twickenham, with the whole proceeds devoted to charity. It would certainly prove a crowd-puller and I'm quite sure the players themselves would welcome it with open arms.

Not that I think we will ever see such a match come to pass, for the feud between Union and League is far too bitter and deep-rooted to allow for any such fraternization, either now or in the near future. That it should be so is, in my view, mainly the fault of the Rugby Union people.

As I said at the outset of this chapter, the Union authorities can never be blamed for seeking to maintain the amateur code as a separate entity. Not content with that, however, they seem for ever to be seeking ways and means of keeping the feud alive and active. Every so often there are instances of former professional players who have returned to South Wales and elsewhere being ordered out of clubs where they have been introduced as guests by their former Union pals and colleagues.

From a personal viewpoint, these stories cause me no misgivings whatsoever, for there are plenty of athletic and social clubs in which I am welcome, without visiting any wherein I am possibly not, but they do unfortunately smack of a desire to keep the embers of this age-old controversy actively alight. If Sir Leonard Hutton, Denis Compton, Stanley Matthews, Dai Rees, or any other prominent sportsman was introduced as a guest to, say, the Cardiff or Harlequin clubs, they would, and rightly so, be welcomed with open arms. Why the same welcome should not exist for a celebrity whose chosen professional sport happens to be rugby football is beyond the comprehension of a good many people besides myself.

Another inconsistency in the Rugby Union attitude is observed in their refusal to let the Rugby League touring sides from New Zealand and Australia make use of the Rugby Union ground which adjoins their customary headquarters at Ilkley, Yorkshire. Of course I know full well that the Union have a by-law which prohibits their teams and players making use of a ground regularly used by Rugby League players, but experience has shown that the Union themselves are never loath to make use of a professional ground on those occasions when they want to cram in the greatest possible number of cash customers. I myself have played Rugby Union football at Villa Park, the H.Q. of the famous professional association club, Aston Villa.

Frequently, of course, the anti-Rugby Unionists retaliate by accusing certain Union clubs of under-the-counter payments to their players - accusations which periodically make headlines in the national Press and which, true or untrue, do little service to the game of rugby football. In fact a lot of people are under the impression that the star amateur player does well out of the game financially, so much so that when I was a regular player with Llanelly after my release from the Navy, a good many of my friends took it for granted that I was picking up anything from three pounds to a fiver every week during the rugger season. Had this really been the case, I would possibly have remained an amateur to this day.

This is not to say that some of the more enterprising lads do not work the oracle on their expenses, and I suppose it is true to say, and I'm not speaking only of Wales, there are instances where a club committee has been prepared to be indulgent in these matters. On the whole, though, I'm pretty sure most chaps who have played first-class rugby in Wales will agree with me when I say that you've got to be a very slick talker indeed to extract any illicit cash out of the pocket of the average club treasurer in those parts.

In fact my only opportunity to make any money out of Rugby Union football came after I'd joined the Rugby League, and in the form of an invitation from a Sunday newspaper editor to write a couple of articles exposing the under-the-counter payments in Welsh rugby. I had to pass it by simply because I possessed no first-hand knowledge.

I can't help thinking that in a good many cases it is those who shout loudest about the virtues of amateur sport who make the most out of it financially. I am not referring to players or, for that matter, to the many zealous and sport-loving officials and administrators who give much of their leisure time - and quite frequently money out of their own pockets - in the cause of the game they love. The people I do refer to are those who make a fat living out of amateur sport by writing and broadcasting, and, not content with that, have the audacity to come out in all their pristine purity as the great apostles of amateurism.

Rugby football has a few, and amateur athletics - the most fanatical of them all - a vast horde. Indeed it is my opinion that anyone who commands an income through his connection with any amateur sport has no earthly right to decry professionalism. Meanwhile, as our elders feud and fume over this sixty-three-year-old controversy between the two codes, I and my fellow professionals will continue to maintain and enjoy our frequent contacts and social intercourse with the lads who play the Union game. Neither the legislators or law books, thank goodness, can stop it; nor, I'm sure, ever will.

24

PROBLEM BOY

'Problem Boy' is an epithet that has been applied to me pretty liberally throughout my rugby career, and I am not egotistical enough to believe that it is intended to convey the fact that I sometimes set my opponents problems on the field.

On the contrary I know that the term is used to imply that I am quite often a headache to selectors, and in some cases to the authorities who control the game itself. While I am ready to agree that there have been occasions when my form has been wayward enough to present problems for selection committees, I cannot recall a single occasion on which I have gone out of my way purposely to flaunt authority. That is why I can truthfully say that the furore that arose up North over my non-selection for the 1958 British team to tour Australia came as a complete shock to me.

Let me recap on a story that made headlines throughout the Northern Press. The events leading up to this major controversy were as I give them. Following my return from the unsuccessful World Cup venture in Australia during the summer of 1957, I recommenced playing for Leeds in the August and straight away, although I say it myself, hit - and what's more maintained - the best form I had struck since turning professional.

In his heart, every player knows, or should know, when he is playing well, and certainly I was well satisfied with my form throughout the winter of 1957-8. Although I wasn't setting up any new records my defence had tightened up considerably, whilst unlike previous seasons I was consistent. Yet I failed to impress the Rugby League selectors who, quite within their rights, omitted me from every representative match played that winter - the three Tests with France, and the three special tour trials.

It was, as things turned out, my omission from the last of these representative games - the third and final tour trial at Headingley - that really started things going. It was then that the *Yorkshire Evening News* Rugby League writer, Arthur Haddock, produced his famous 'Smear story' in which he alleged that the reason for my omission from representative games, far from having any connection with actual football playing, was due to the fact that I had offended authority by speaking out of turn during the World Cup series in Australia the previous summer. That did it. In next to no time I found myself beleaguered by all manner of people, some of them perfect strangers, all anxious to hear my views on Arthur Haddock's sensational story.

Naturally I refrained from comment at the time, because to begin with there was not a great deal, as far as I was concerned, to comment on; besides, the Rugby League Selectors had not finally committed themselves to a definite list of players to tour 'Down Under'. That condition, of course, no longer applies now, so in so far as I am able I feel free to answer the many questions asked of me at the time.

First, was Arthur Haddock's story substantially true? My answer to that is that I never knew Arthur write anything that was untrue. Second question: Have you any idea in what way you've offended authority? Answer: I can only go upon the evidence of friends in the newspaper world who tell me that a remark I made to a fellow player following the match in which we were defeated by Australia was relayed to the team manager who, apparently, regarded it as defeatist talk, if not downright treason.

The remark - 'You only play hard to get here' - implying of course that the only part that interested me was getting my aeroplane ticket to Australia and that the rest was, as far as I was concerned, just a picnic-cum-vacation. Obviously readers will want to know whether I actually did make a comment of this nature. I can only say that I cannot honestly recall, even in a jocular mood, ever making a remark of this nature to anyone. I might add, though, that I have my own views on this particular subject. Publication of them here or anywhere else will not do anyone any good, however, least of all the game of Rugby League. Sufficient then to say that for the first and only time in my six and a half years in Rugby League I encountered petty jealousy and malice, but, thank goodness, only from two persons.

As most people know, I failed to make my third Australian tour under League auspices, and naturally I was disappointed. Although it is a big wrench being separated from one's family so frequently, I, and I'm sure the majority of Rugby League players, regard the honour as well worth the pangs of partings and home-sickness.

Perhaps this is as good a time as any to pay a tribute to my own wife Maureen. I'm certain she typifies the majority of football wives, in the sense that she lives for the game of Rugby League as intensely, in many ways more so, than I do myself. There are, in fact, few 'rugby widows' in the League, for almost without exception the wives attend the matches, and their active support and encouragement does not end there; far from it.

In my own case, I lean on Maureen even more heavily than I am sometimes prepared to admit to her personally. Injuries, loss of form, nervous tension and oftentimes controversy, are some of the things a rugby wife has to contend with, for there is no escaping the fact that these things affect them to almost the same degree as they do their husbands. Maureen has borne them all cheerfully, and only once in fact have I seen her hopping mad over rugby football. That was when our young son Kevin accompanied me down to Headingley on an early season training session, and followed me into the showers - with his clothes on! I can tell you my ears fairly blistered as a result of that one.

Encouragement of their own menfolk apart, the 'Merry Wives' of Leeds (as a newspaper article once referred to them) play a not inconsiderable part in fostering the team spirit of which Headingley is so proud, for they have formed their own very exclusive club, exclusive that is as far as the menfolk are concerned. Every week, on a rota system, one wife acts as hostess to the others, and although one cannot rightly suppose that they work out Saturday's tactics over their knitting and innumerable cups of tea, their social activities do undoubtedly make for a happy all-round atmosphere at Headingley. Indeed, the club recognized the fact by inviting them all down to London at Cup Final week-end, and it was fitting that the celebration should be a victory one.

Rugby football apart, I like nothing better than to relax by my own fireside, or else pottering about the house itself. I can't say that I'm an expert 'do it yourself' character, but I do nevertheless enjoy doing jobs of this description about the home. Mind you, my enthusiasm in this direction has often landed me in far more tricky and complicated situations than I have ever encountered on a football field! On several occasions during my handyman's career I've reached the point of 'no return' - the point at which, having torn up half the floor, and huge chunks out of the wall, you simply have to go through with the job or else call in the experts. It's a dicey business, I can tell you.

In the outdoor line, I have a passion for motor-cars, and though my opportunities for playing have been somewhat limited owing to injuries, and tours abroad, I still retain a keen interest in cricket, and a day in the sun watching Yorkshire play at Headingley is something I enjoy very much indeed. My own private cricket hero incidentally is Fred Trueman, whom I admire intensely both as an individual and a cricketer. In fact, I'd rather be able to bowl like Fred than beat Rugby League records at goal-kicking. Despite the criticism that has come his way in the past there is no more sincere or warm-hearted sportsman playing than this very fine Yorkshire fast bowler. Brian Close, too, is another great favourite of mine, and Headingley is never a dull place when he or Fred are out there in the middle.

My career as a Rugby League professional has enabled me to meet all manner of personalities famous in other sporting fields: Ray Lindwall, Keith Miller, Raich Carter, my own countrymen John Charles and Dai Rees, and to my mind at least the most unforgettable of them all - Stanley Matthews. Added to his unique ability as a footballer is a natural kindliness and unassuming bearing under circumstances.

Of all the trophies I've collected during my sporting career, the one I treasure the most is a pair of light-weight boots given to me by 'the master' when we were working together on an advertising campaign. Another really unassuming character was John Charles, an idol in Leeds before he left to play for the Italian club Juventus.

25

THE PRESS

The Press, with a few exceptions - chiefly in my native South Wales - have always been extraordinarily kind to me, not only as regards their criticism of my footballing, but in many instances as valued friends and advisers off the field.

Let me be perfectly frank and say that this book itself would have taken probably a lifetime to compile had it not been for the invaluable assistance and advice of some very good friends, one of them being a journalist and fellow Welshman, J.R. Jones, who incidentally played at stand-off half for Hull Rugby League club before he started to write on the game for the *Herald of Wales*.

Mention of J.R.'s footballing career causes me to recall the countless occasions on which I've heard players resent Press criticism on the grounds that 'the writer had never played the game himself.' If you took a census of dressing-room opinion I think you would find that the majority of players subscribe to the view that practical experience as a footballer is an essential prelude to writing about the game. It is not, I might say, a viewpoint that I endorse completely, for experience has shown that the best players are not of necessity the best coaches, or selectors, so by the same token why should it be assumed that they make the best writers?

Obviously the millennium would be an erudite and stylish piece of criticism written by an ex-player of international repute, but the inescapable fact is that the man who can rip a defence apart with a brilliant side-step is not, in most instances, quite so deft with a pen in his hand. I don't know of many literary stylists who could cope with a 'stiff-arm' tackle.

Altogether I think it would be fair to say that the majority of rugby writers who have not in their younger days been active performers have, in most cases, a genuine love and enthusiasm for the game, and that these qualities and a lifetime's experience of watching the game and writing about it have made them wise and knowledgeable critics.

I exclude from this, of course, the 'angle' boys who, presumably at the dictate of their editors, are more concerned about what you had for breakfast than the whys and wherefores of your good or bad games. This quest for 'the story behind the match' can produce some really nauseating writing.

During my days as a Llanelly player we travelled over to play Bath with a rather depleted fifteen which made my brother Alun, who was captaining the side, express some doubt as to the outcome. As things turned out, Bath were not so hot themselves, and since I was able to kick a bagful of goals we won rather more easily than was expected. However, what was even more unexpected than the victory, and certainly not as welcome, was the absolutely nauseating 'sob story' that was spread over the back page of one of the national newspapers on the Monday morning.

King of Rugger

According to the writer my brother Alun had been absolutely distraught with worry all through the train journey to Bath and was apparently on the point of ending it all with a dive out of the compartment window, when kid brother Lewis cheeped in with the remark, 'Don't worry, Alun, I've brought my kicking-boots with me today - the ones I scored nineteen points with for the Barbarians against Penarth last season.' Then the writer went on to relate how my encouragement had acted like a charm on Alun and the rest of the boys, and how things turned out as prophesied.

I don't know much about the ins and outs of newspapers, but I can't help wondering whether editors do in fact seriously believe that this kind of drivel appeals to real rugby lovers. Or is it, I wonder, that the women readers outnumber the male, for I'm convinced it is only a female who could stomach such 'pansy' stuff as the piece I've just quoted. I am glad to say that this kind of stuff is not the normal diet of Rugby League or Rugby Union, for both codes are adorned by writers who can compare with the very greatest in any game.

Greatest of them all in Rugby Union football certainly is, to my mind, Vivian Jenkins of the *Sunday Times*. His most entertaining style of writing can be better appreciated for the knowledge that he was, in his day, one of the very greatest of international full-backs. Vivian does not spare criticism where it is justified, but it is always good-humoured criticism and as such tempered with a deep appreciation and understanding of the moods, problems, and pitfalls of football and footballers.

Pre-eminent in the Rugby League is, in my opinion, Alfred Drewry of the *Yorkshire Post*, who has spent a lifetime watching and writing about the Rugby League game and indeed shows it in every sentence he writes about it. Other very able writers from the rugby angle are Tom Longworth

(*News Chronicle*), John Bapty (*Yorkshire Evening Post*), Arthur Haddock (*Yorkshire Evening News*), Leslie Tremlett (*Evening Chronicle*), Phil King (*People*), and Dereck Marshall (*Daily Mail*), whilst Eddie Waring, whose sometimes pungent comments in the *Sunday Pictorial* makes him perhaps more enemies than most, cannot be accused of not knowing his stuff, nor indeed of being afraid to express his viewpoint.

In Wales, where you might expect the standard of Rugby Union reporting and writing to be highest, it is surprisingly enough rather mediocre - mainly, I suppose, because the city of Cardiff exercises a virtual monopoly of the newspaper scene in its national aspects. Bryn Thomas, the rugby correspondent of Wales's leading daily newspaper, the *Western Mail*, is a sound and knowledgeable critic whose writings reveal that he has made a deep study of the game and its tactics. His reports, too, are an absolute model of accuracy, for he seldom fails to pinpoint the correct player involved - even in a movement that has begun and ended in a few split seconds. When you've mentioned Bryn Thomas and the two West Wales correspondents, Ron Griffiths of the *Swansea Evening Post*, and J.R. Jones of the *Herald of Wales*, however, you have for all practical purposes fully covered the worthwhile aspects of Welsh rugby writing.

Many writers 'plug' their favourite players quite shamelessly, and though the Welsh selectors will argue that they are not influenced by newspaper critics, one sometimes wonders why certain players have been chosen and others overlooked. Roy Sutton was a case in point in 1950. In the final trial at Cardiff, Roy scored a couple of tries on the blind side of the scrum, even though his immediate opponent was Ray Cale - the greatest blind-side wing-forward of his era. Yet despite this, and his undisputed brilliance in club football throughout the winter, Roy was ignored by the Welsh Selectors.

King of Rugger

I suppose it is really only human that writers should lean towards the players they see most frequently in action, and since it so happens that the majority of the national daily representatives are based in Cardiff, their criticisms should have an Eastern bias - even if unintentionally.

I once heard a priceless story concerning a rugby writer who, in the days before the last war, was responsible for covering the activities of one of the leading clubs in West Wales. During the week in which a Welsh fifteen was due to be picked he staggered the rugby world with the suggestion that twelve players from the club he followed deserved selection in the national side. This, it seems, was rather too much for the constitution of one of the officials of a rival club, who expressed his disapproval somewhat as follows: 'One certainly, perhaps tow, or even three, but, play the game, twelve is absolutely beyond all reason surely?' To this our particular scribe replied, 'It's all very well for you to talk, but back at X' (the club he wrote about) 'they want to know what's wrong with the three players I haven't put forward for caps' - from which it appears that it's not all honey being a rugby critic. Not in Wales, anyway.

In the final analysis, however, the virtues of the British Press far outweighs its bad points. Indeed rugby football, whether League or Union, would be in a pretty poor way without it and, speaking as a player, I think most of us have been indebted at one time or another to the Press boys for their vigilance and for the alacrity with which they are ever ready to play their part in both exposing and securing redress for some of the injustices that are sometimes perpetrated in secret. You can take it from me that were it not for the presence and watchfulness of the Press, there would be some pretty queer things done in the name of 'Sport'.

26

THE ARSENAL OF THE RUGBY LEAGUE

The Arsenal Football Club, one of the legends incidentally of my schooldays, may have shed some of its former glamour, and, perhaps, a little of its prestige, but it still ranks amongst the aristocracy of association football.

I like to think that if this great club possesses a counterpart in Rugby League, then it is my own club, Leeds. I don't think that is an extravagant claim, for many times I've heard even the more partisan supporters of other Rugby League clubs admit that the Leeds club are ever popular visitors to their grounds. Perhaps an important reason is that, win or lose, in lean cycles or on the crest of success, the Headingley Club seldom deviate from their long-established policy of playing open and attractive rugby.

As with the Arsenal in their palmiest days, Leeds have always been prepared to spend lavishly in an effort to attract the stars from overseas and elsewhere to their ranks, and this, too, has made them a great drawing card in the League.

King of Rugger

Indeed the Arsenal parallel is in all respects a pretty close one, for like the famous association club, the Leeds club regard only the best as good enough for Headingley, and by the same token regard themselves as honour bound to extend only the best of treatment to those players fortunate to join them. Certainly, and even at the risk of appearing maudlin, I'll say here and now that I am as proud to have worn the blue and amber jersey as of any other honour I've been fortunate enough to obtain at rugby football.

It all started, according to the history books, way back in 1890 when a local church team called St John's were invited to form the rugby football section of the Leeds Cricket, Football and Athletic Co., which had just taken over the tenancy of the newly constructed Headingley ground. St John's was a Rugby Union team, incidentally clad in the present Leeds colours of blue and amber, who played their first match at Headingley on September 20th, 1890, against another famous name of an old and largely forgotten era - the Bradford club, Manningham. In 1895 came the famous 'broken-time' dispute which resulted in twenty Northern clubs breaking away from the Rugby Union over the question of payments for time and wages lost as a result of playing rugby football. Thus there came into being, and on an entirely professional basis, the Northern Union, later renamed the Rugby League, of which St John's, by now also renamed (Leeds), were founder members.

Doughty competitors in the old Northern Union (they were Challenge Cup winners in 1910, and Championship runners-up in 1915), the Leeds club really came into its own with the reconstitution of the Rugby League in 1922 and it was, I'm assured, no coincidence that the club's emergence as a real power in the game coincided with the appointment of Sir Edwin Airey as Chairman of the Headingley Company in 1923.. Sir Edwin reigned for over thirty years, and his vision and enterprise became a byword almost universally. Under his leadership Leeds began to look far and wide for the stars who could pack Headingley. From Australia came Dinny Campbell, Jeff Moores, Frank O'Rourke, Joe Busch, and in the person of Eric Harris the most famously remembered of them all.

Time and again I've listened to the old men of Headingley recount the wonderful exploits of this super wing-man whose trick of leaving opposing full-backs grasping thin air with a surge of extra pace earned him the nickname of the 'Toowoomba Ghost'. In his nine seasons at Headingley Harris established all kinds of records, including the club record of sixty-three tries which still stands to this day. Australia, in fact, has always done proudly by Leeds. Although the war came to interrupt the career of Vic Hey I've been told that he was one of the most powerful centre three-quarters who ever played in the League. Then in my own time were the fine Australian players, Keith McLellan, who captained us at Wembley, Arthur Clues, Ken Kearney, Bruce Ryan, Ted Verrenkamp, and that most colourful of all Headingley characters, Bob McMaster.

My own country, Wales, has done quite well by Headingley, for it has supplied the club with many famous players beginning with Frank Young of Cardiff, who kicked seven goals in the 1910 Cup Final, Willie Bowen (Swansea), W.A. Davies and Evan Williams (both of Aberavon), J.F. Thompson and Con Murphy (Cross Keys), Iorrie Isaacs (Cardiff), and Dickie Ralph (Newport). Then nearer my own time there have been men of the calibre of Cliff Evans (Neath), Ike Owens and Billy Banks (Maesteg), Gareth Price (Llanelly), Idwal Davies (Swansea), Dickie Williams (Mountain Ash), Tommy Cornelius (Cilfynydd), Dai Jenkins (Treherbert), and Dai Prosser (Neath). New Zealand, in the person of H.E. 'Bert' Cooke, provided one of Headingley's greatest ever, of course, for not only was this former Kiwi tourist one of the best full-backs in the game, he was a deadly accurate goal-kicker as well. In six seasons with Leeds, Bert scored 1,169 points - 1,112 of them from goal kicks.

Lest anyone should run away with the idea that Leeds have been exclusively a League of Nations outfit, let me hasten to add that some of the club's home-produced products have established their own special niche in the game's history, amongst them the celebrated Joe Thompson, who led the club to victory in the 1932 Cup Final against Swinton at Wigan. During his career of eleven seasons with the club he scored 1,883 points - a record that, for all the success I've obtained, has yet to be surpassed. Then there was Les Adams, a fine scrum half, Stanley Smith a free-scoring wing-man, and the immortal Stanley Brogden.

Another Headingley player whose name comes immediately into any discussion of the great figures of the past is that of Jim Brough, nowadays back in his native Cumberland, managing Workington Town. Jim was at his best as a full-back during the heyday of Jim Sullivan, and the rivalry between them was intense. While many of the old-timers will concede Sullivan the mastery at goal-kicking, they will not have it that the great Welshman could show Brough anything when it came to punting a rugger ball.

On the subject of Leeds home-spun material, I'm sure this is an opportune moment to point out that of the side that triumphed at Wembley in 1957 no fewer than eight - Del Hodgkinson, George Broughton, Jack Lendill, Jeff Stevenson, Joe Anderson, Bernard Prior, Don Robinson, and Harry Street - were native-born Yorkshiremen, whilst five - Hodgkinson, Broughton, Lendill, Prior, and Stevenson - were products of Leeds schoolboy football. That, I think, should silence the scoffers who sometimes declare that Headingley buy their success.

The Arsenal Of The Rugby League

Oddly enough, Leeds, for all their great success previously in other directions, including the Challenge Cup and Yorkshire Cup competitions, have never as yet won the Rugby League Championship. Five times Leeds have reached the final, only to falter at the post, and even the club's statisticians have lost count of the times the blue and ambers have appeared in the Championship semi-finals. Critics and fans alike have often expressed themselves at a loss to explain a failure that has persisted throughout the years, even at such times as when the club has been sweeping the decks in other competitions.

With only half a dozen seasons' service to my credit, I am naturally hesitant about putting forward my own views on a subject that has baffled more knowledgeable and experienced critics, but my own private theory is that any side which goes in for the open and all-out attacking game - the predominant feature of the club's football down the years - must always be vulnerable to opponents who are prepared to sit back and wait for the inevitable mistake. There are, of course, many such opponents in Rugby League football, and the higher the stakes, the more determined they become to let the other side do the leading. That is why, in my view anyhow, Leeds have so often been unexpectedly defeated at the very last hurdle. Still, I'm sure this aura of unpredictability adds to the charm of watching Leeds in action and, if it comes to that, I seriously doubt whether our own Headingley followers would have it any other way. I know for a fact that when, a few winters ago, skipper Arthur Clues decided that some strong concentrated forward play might help to offset some transparent weaknesses behind the scrum, the Headingley followers recoiled from the spectacle as though someone had swapped, overnight as it were, their beloved Rugby League for American rugby or Australian Rules football.

Indeed, if Leeds were to obtain a whole string of victories by strong-arm methods, I'm pretty sure we should soon be playing before empty stands and terraces, for Headingley followers have been brought up to expect the very best both in material and achievement and they are accordingly quick to recognize and even quicker to voice their disapproval of the second-rate or ersatz. If in fact these warmhearted and knowledgeable Headingley supporters have a fault, it is that they sometimes tend to be hypercritical, and unfortunately the person who invariably has to bear the brunt of almost everyone's displeasure when things go wrong is team manager and coach Ken Dalby. Ironically enough, he is the very person responsible for Leeds' great standing in the world of Rugby League.

I have referred to Ken many times before in the course of this book, and I make no apology for doing so again for he has been a great friend and adviser, both to me personally and to countless other players who have arrived somewhat diffidently at Headingley. We are, of course, fortunate that we have a real live and active board of directors headed by the chairman, Mr. George Airey, who, like his father before him, simply lives the cause of Leeds rugby, but in the main it is Ken Dalby who guides the destiny of the club in the place it matters most - on the field of play. Ken does not suffer fools gladly, and he is a hard man to deceive, which means that not every player sees eye to eye with him on every occasion. Yet nothing that Ken Dalby asks of a player can ever be deemed lacking in shrewd common sense, and in his every action or edict there is abundant evidence of a genuine and selfless love and enthusiasm for rugby football; the rugby football of Leeds above all.

Ken was a schoolmaster before taking up his coaching and managerial post at Headingley, and often during training sessions this fact is brought home to us. Although he has long since dispensed with the cane and blackboard, he remains a tireless mentor of the game's moves and its theory. What's more important, you feel impelled to listen - invariably with profit. Those two stalwart Australians, Arthur Clues and Bob McMaster, were certainly helped by the tact and shrewdness of the Leeds manager. They were colourful characters, these two outsize Australian forwards, and tough ones into the bargain. Bob McMaster, in fact, not content with a Saturday afternoon stint in the Leeds front row, used to fill in his evenings with All-In Wrestling round the halls.

When I toured Australia for the second time in 1954, I met Bob at his native Brisbane. He had finished with football by then, and his main complaint was that the 'Wrestling' racket in Australia was a 'closed shop'. Arthur Clues, the greatest of 'cobbers' to me at Headingley, had perhaps rather more finesse than Bob, though not so much that our opponents would notice. He was one of the finest second-row forwards I have seen in any class of football, and in one aspect at least - his side-stepping ability - quite the greatest forward ever. For a man of fifteen stone Arthur was incredibly light, and I imagine that his side-step must have come out of the very same drawer as that which contained Bleddyn William's.

Another great figure at Headingley when I first arrived there was my fellow countryman Dickie Williams, under whose captaincy (he was a Hunslet player then) I later toured Australia. Dickie, who hailed from Mountain Ash, was a comparative unknown when he joined Leeds in 1946, but he soon emerged as the natural successor to Willy Davies in the Welsh international side. He was one of the smallest players in the League but, over a short distance, probably one of the fastest as well. I must confess that were I to do justice to all the fine players and personalities I've encountered at Headingley alone, then I would have to approach the publishers on the question of a second volume.

As it is I'll wind this chapter up by quoting the words of Ken Dalby in the souvenir brochure that marked our appearance at Wembley: 'This is a great club, and a happy one' - a sentiment that I echo from the bottom of my heart.

27

THEY COULD BEAT THE WORLD

It has been a long road from the village ground at Gorseinon, where I first acquired my interest in rugby football, to Wembley Stadium on Cup Final day, to the clamour and excitement of the Sydney Cricket Ground on the occasion of a Test match between Great Britain and Australia.

On the way I have played the game of rugby football in all manner of conditions and against a wide variety of opponents, yet I can honestly say that I have experienced nothing that has served to alter my conviction that, potentially at least, my own country, Wales, is the greatest rugby nation of them all. I am confident that I am being neither arrogant nor unduly partisan when I say that Wales could beat the world were only her vast natural resources marshalled properly and to the full.

To begin with history supports me in the view. Welshmen have a natural aptitude for this game of rugby, an aptitude only too well illustrated by the fact that the game's

'Hall of Fame' contains the names of so many who have worn the scarlet jersey with the three feathers - Trew, Owen, Bush, Gould, Nicholls, Bancroft, Vile, Morgan, Llewelyn, Rowe Harding, Wick Powell, Claude Davey, Cliff Jones, Wilf Wooller, Willy Davies, Hadyn Tanner, 'Bunner' Travers, Ken Jones, Cliff Morgan, Bleddyn Williams ... the list is in fact inexhaustible. Then if you want further proof of the Welshman's aptitude for the game, you have it first of all in the fact that ever since professional rugby began its sponsors have been looking to South Wales as a prolific source of stars as well as raw material. Secondly, a Rugby Union touring team seldom leaves these shores without containing a strong leavening, and in most cases a majority, of Welshmen.

Aptitude and ability apart, however, is it not a fact that in Wales we probably play *more* really organized rugby than in any other country, save possibly those of New Zealand and South Africa?

The latter countries do not play anything like the same amount of *first-class* rugby as we do. Certainly neither England, Ireland, Scotland, France nor Australia can claim the same intense interest and enthusiasm that features the Welsh game from the schoolboy stage and upwards. We have junior and secondary schools rugby, youth rugby, second- and first-class rugby, all run on a properly graded basis. Altogether there must be several thousand players in action every Saturday afternoon.

Up to a few years ago our schoolboy and secondary schools' XVs. could usually administer both a start and a licking to their counterparts in the other countries. The fact that they don't still do so I'll explain later, but in the meantime I think I've put forward sufficient arguments to justify my confirmed opinion that Wales should win the Triple Crown and International Championship far oftener than they actually do.

They Could Beat The World

The fact that they *do not* has, I suggest, nothing at all to do with either rugby skill, tactics, or techniques; leastways, not in the first place. I confidently state that the greatest hindrance to the success of Wales in international rugby will be found in her constitutional set-up. For administrative purposes Welsh rugby is split up into districts, with the district representatives appointed by ballot - the voting being done by the affiliated clubs within that district. Once elected, the district representatives form the full Welsh Union Committee and straight away meet to appoint from amongst themselves the various sub-committees that are necessary. This is where the trouble really begins, for among the sub-committees elected is one of the most important - the Selection Committee - and I am not alone in the view that the procedure is detrimental to Welsh rugby.

Under ideal circumstances the members of a selection committee, any selection committee, should be completely neutral in outlook and, to that end, absolutely divorced from the game's administration and politics. Alas, under the Welsh set-up this, I'm afraid, is impossible, for as unbiased as a Selector may try to be he can never lose sight (nor is he often allowed to) of the fact that he owes his seat on the Union to the whim and indulgence of the clubs who have voted for him. The evils of the system are obvious, and it is to my mind equally obvious that there have been cases of Welsh selectors placating their electorate by championing the cause of players on purely parochial grounds. Indeed, the history of Welsh rugby is full of 'one-cap players' of whom many, of course, have been just 'unlucky'. Another difficulty that confronts a Welsh selector is that, in common with the rest of the Union members, he has to go cap in hand to ask for re-election every season, which could mean that in his brief year of office a selector is more concerned with producing immediate results than with team-building on a long-term basis. Altogether, I'm sure that the answer lies in the Welsh selection committee being:

(1) Appointed from outside the Union itself.
(2) Extended the security of, say, three years in office.

I have, I might add, learnt that the Welsh Union in 1958 amended their laws (under pressure of public opinion) to allow for the co-option on its selection committee of a person outside the Union, but that I think was more in the nature of a sop to public opinion than a genuine effort to bring about a long overdue reform.

Another criticism I have to make of Welsh selectors is that they tend to be unreasonably conservative in outlook. At one time or another you've all heard the tag, 'It's easier to get into the Welsh fifteen than out of it'. I'm not going to say that this is literally true, but they always seemed to me loath to overlook reputations. I recall only too well how odd selectors used to come into the dressing-room before trial matches and say, 'Don't forget, lads, reputations don't count today, so play your hardest.' It didn't mean a thing really, and what's more nearly everyone knew it. Inasmuch as I obtained my own cap on the basis of a trial match, you might think I'm being somewhat uncharitable, but don't forget that in 1950 Wales had no established 'name' as a candidate for the full-back position and they were hard up for a goal-kicker too.

There are, of course, outstanding exceptions to every rule, but by and large I'm of the opinion that as far as Welsh international XVs. are concerned player-official relations could do with a great deal of improving. Not even in professional rugby, where you would expect the atmosphere to be less cordial, have I encountered the autocracy, and on occasions downright rudeness, that often featured the Welsh official attitude to the fellows who did the actual playing.

So much then for the administrative side of the game in Wales, and even though of course its conduct is open to criticism you cannot justly claim that it is wholly responsible for Wales's sometime lack-lustre efforts in international rugby. Personally I feel that Welsh XVs. more often that not fall short of the high expectations of their followers for no other reason that in the majority of international matches they fall back on tactics and techniques that are utterly foreign, not only to the Welsh tradition down the years, but also to their normal habit.

I once overheard the Irish captain, Des O'Brien, sum it all up in really admirable fashion. As you probably recall, Des spent the latter part of his career playing for Cardiff, although he was still captaining Ireland in the international arena. Playing alongside people like Cliff Morgan, Bleddyn Williams, Gareth Griffiths, Alun Thomas, and the rest one Saturday - and due to play against them for Ireland on the following - Des used to spend the intervening week pondering how on earth his Irish team would be able to find the counter to the brilliant skill and baffling unorthodoxy these players habitually produced in Welsh club football. In most cases, however, Des's fears were groundless for, as he put it, 'once these chaps had exchanged a Cardiff jersey for a Welsh one they more often than not became different players - ordinary, orthodox, and seemingly weighed down with anxiety'. To my mind, that applies not only to Bleddyn and the rest, but to all Welsh players, myself very often included, during international matches. Instead of using the gifts that nature has so freely endowed us with - speed, guile, and an instinct to attack - we worried overmuch about what the other side might do, or not do, and paid too much attention to tactical theories. In general we concentrated on a policy of safety first, and the rest afterwards.

King of Rugger

Wales, I fancy, have, in the rugby sense, been unduly influenced by the gospel of concentrated forward play that has come across the sea from New Zealand and South Africa. When Ireland won the Triple Crown two years running with a modified version of this strategy just after the war we fell hook, line, and sinker for the new mode in international rugby, meanwhile forgetting that other things being equal good backs will always win a match. In this respect, a whole lot of people seem to subscribe to the view that Wales won her two Triple Crowns under John Gwilliam solely on the merit of strong concentrated forward play, but, believe me, they're making a great mistake. Our forwards' ability to out-scrum and out-ruck the opposition was, I'll grant, the basis of that success, but John Gwilliam was far too astute a captain even to attempt making his pack the main striking arm as well as the reconnaissance unit of his fighting force. The striking force in fact were the backs, and once the forwards had gained the vital ascendancy, Gwilliam saw to it that they were utilized to the full - as indeed he had to, for it would have been worse than stupidity to dispense with formidable skill, power, and speed merely on the altar of some tactical theory.

In retrospect I'm quite certain that had Cliff Morgan, in the pivotal position behind the Welsh scrum, played the same type of game against South Africa as he did in the same season at Twickenham and Dublin, then we would have defeated the Springboks and maybe in the process put and end to this talk of forward play as the be-all and end-all of rugby football. I will instantly agree, of course, that employment of the backs must be conditional on at least an equality forward, but I am sure it need be no more than an equality. And I am equally sure that Wales should trust more to her backs in international football in preference to (as she so often does) embarking on a forward campaign just because it happens to be the fashion.

During the last couple of years I have heard that Wales

are experiencing a marked shortage of top-class backs, particularly centres and wings. This, I am sure, can only be because the unreasonable emphasis on forward play that has featured international football for so much of the post-war period has been carried into club football, with the result that the potentially brilliant attacking player is being denied the opportunity to develop his gifts. It is indeed nonsense to say that Welsh rugby cannot continue to flourish on the merit of the swift skillful back play that made its name a household one wherever the game was played - nonsense because Cardiff have continued to achieve really outstanding success with football of this kind right through the post-war epoch. One might really say that the sheer brilliance of their backs have time and again been able to offset the deficiencies of the club pack, and I see no reason to prevent Wales being able to do the same.

If I seem to criticise the rugby of my own country somewhat harshly, then please believe me when I say that I only do so out of a desire to see it take its rightful place as one of the real powers in the game. From my travels in New Zealand, Australia, South Africa, and France, I have learnt how much people of other countries honour and respect our reputation in rugby matters, and I for one would like to keep it that way.

If I may close on a personal note, Welsh rugby has been good to me right from the time I kicked my first football at Gorseinon. Its people, critics, followers, and friends alike have been kind towards me. Thus whatever its imperfections, it will always be the closest thing to my heart - and I mean no disrespect to my many friends who in their various ways have helped me to enjoy a career that has been truly international. I thank you one and all for helping me, if nothing else, to the knowledge that in the last analysis true friendship knows not the bounds of either codes or nationalities.

King of Rugger

AFTERWORD
By Lewis Jones
2008

So there you have it: my autobiography. Well, up to a point, anyway. For life - and a rugby career - moves on. Results after the Challenge Cup victory in '57 were nothing much to write home about, but 1961 turned out to be the highlight of my years with Leeds when, bingo, I was privileged to captain the club to their first ever Championship success.

With the present-day Leeds Rhinos side reaching Grand Finals regularly, it might not appear that special now. But after a near seventy-year wait for the top honour, winning the Championship was massive for the Headingley officials, us players, the city and, of course, the Leeds fans.

For so long the Loiners had been regarded as a top side, one with a great Cup tradition, but what was lacking was the game-wide respect that comes with winning the title; the ultimate measure of consistency. We were paid £32 for the win over Warrington that secured the coveted prize, but I don't think any of us gave that a single thought. We all loved coach Dai Prosser but, even though he was instrumental in the spirit engendered amongst the side, he was shown the door. I am sure that the powers-that-be were subsequently embarrassed, but they had negotiated with Roy Francis – the best coach in the game – to come to Headingley and take over the following season.

I played under Roy for three years and he worked us hard. But the result was the best Leeds team that I have ever seen, combining the talents of youngsters I watched come in and develop, like Mick Shoebottom and Alan Smith, with some terrific experienced players. By the late 1960s, Roy had added the likes of John Atkinson, Syd Hynes and then Les Dyl, who prospered alongside the proven abilities of Tony Fisher and Bob Haigh - one of the best second-rowers I ever saw - and one of the last ball-playing loose forwards, Ray Batten.

Our form that title-winning season was a one-off. We'd been a mid-table side before that and we put together a run of wins that began to instill a real belief among us. We kept being told that we'd had an easier fixture run, but beating St. Helens at home in a thunderous semi - when I had a wonderful duel with the great Alex Murphy - and then Warrington in the final, proved that we were deserved winners.

Thinking back, there were a few that I played with in and around that time that I'd put in a personal 'World Class' select. Arthur Clues would be the first; he was on his own. I was part of an 'Other Nationalities' side that was possibly the best collection I ever played in and the second-rowers were Aussies: Harry Bath - who was with Warrington - and Cluesy. They were the finest combination in those positions that I ever saw. Of course, my scrum-half would be Jeff Stevenson. He was sensational and the other one who wore blue and amber who couldn't be bettered was Kenny Thornett, the best full-back I witnessed. Others would have come close to selection but that gang were incomparable in my eyes.

In the Championship-winning side, I partnered fellow Welshman Colin Evans at half-back. He was the hardest bloke I ever knew. Colin wouldn't think twice about running into a brick wall if that was what he was asked to do, he was incredibly tough. He might not have been as sophisticated as Jeff but, if you needed minding, he was a handy guy to have around.

In 1960, I started to contemplate what I might do in my retirement after rugby, and I have fond memories of Carnegie, the forerunner of Leeds Met University, where a number of the current Leeds players have just graduated with degrees.

My wife, Maureen, who did not deserve the husband who lacked ambition, ran the confectionery and tobacconist shop we had at West Park, while I was satisfied in various employments, including a pub in Cardigan Road and even selling cars at one stage. With no particular future in store, she persuaded me to enrol on a teacher training course at James Graham College for mature students. It was one of the best things I ever did and I qualified after completing three years of taking mathematics classes in a High School.

Both the '57 Cup and '61 Championship teams broke up pretty quickly, which was a sadness; only Don Robinson and myself survived and were winners in each. In the space of three seasons, that was a high turnover. Don was too much of a gentleman, a terrific player but a different sort to Jack Fairbank. You can't compare him or Dennis Goodwin to the likes of the guys in those positions today. It was a different time that required a different idea of professionalism.

Jack used to turn up in his long brown coat that he'd been milking his cows in since four o'clock in the morning on his family farm, up near Huddersfield. He'd come down to training and turn up at the match dressed like that, in his wellies and with string around his waist, but that was how it was in those days. The rules were different among the forwards. It was a literal battle for supremacy and guys like Jack thrived on that. Every team had its characters. For a while, Garry Hemmingway looked as though he would make a real impact, scoring a lot of tries on the wing, but retiring after suffering a serious injury that saw his star wane. Mind you, he was often in a world of his own. He was very fast, but I don't think he often realised that he was playing in front of a crowd of twenty or thirty thousand. He was more likely to be gazing up at the pigeons in the North Stand roof.

We did capture a Yorkshire Cup between the Wembley and title successes and there were a few Yorkshire Leagues along the way, but if I'm asked about what I won, it can only really be measured by the big two trophies. I was once debating the majesty of Arthur Clues with someone, and I could not believe that one of the all-time greats had no domestic honours from his time here at Leeds. I was sharply reminded that he had a Yorkshire League winner's medal but, to me, that did not really count.

The value of having a profession to fall back on had been brought home to me when, prior to the start of the 1959 campaign, I broke my other arm in a match in Paris, necessitating a plate in that one as well, which was pretty unusual. A French lad, Contrastin, was running down the wing and I'd never thrown a stiff arm in my life but I caught him pretty high as he went past, across the forehead - because he didn't have a neck - and I knew then that it was fatal and the arm was gone; I should have had more sense.

I played on for a few minutes because I didn't want to show that I was hurt by doing something illegal, and then I succumbed. Eventually I went to a hospital in the French capital and the doctor in the casualty department intimated that it was a 'tendon', which he kept repeating while I was shaking my head and telling him it was *cassé*. He wouldn't have it and eventually he just stuck a bandage on it. When I got home, I went to see the surgeon used by Leeds. He had my arm X-rayed and it was badly broken, not fractured. He said: 'you've got a plate in one arm, you might just as well make sure and have the other one done.' I'm sometimes reminded that I rarely gave away a penalty, but that was probably because I wasn't big enough to foul anybody and would probably have been thumped in exchange. There was certainly no dissent. If I was picked up for an indiscretion it was likely to have been for offside, or maybe not playing the ball correctly.

When I was captain up at Leeds, I wasn't one for stirring speeches, tactical discussions or game plans. Nothing like that. We played the game as we saw it. Our only concession was that there were certain key individuals in sides we faced that we didn't want to run riot, but how could you coach or counteract someone like Billy Boston or will-o'-the-wisp Brian Bevan? The opposition would attempt to get the ball to them as often as possible and let their wingers capitalise and we would try to prevent it reaching them. That was about as sophisticated as it got.

Even at Odsal, in the Championship final, our approach to the game didn't change. I had suffered from nerves at Wembley, due to the enormity of the occasion, but there was no real feeling that the weight of over sixty years of Loiners' history was on our shoulders that afternoon. Yes, we were certainly aware of what it meant to everyone connected with the club and the emotion that carried, but all of us just wanted to win that game for its own sake.

There was a lot written and said afterwards about how fitting it was that I should score the final try before going up to collect the elusive silverware, but it was a nothing sort of score. The game was already over and I just happened to be in the right place. My man of the match that afternoon was our hooker, Barry Simms, who stood up in the tackle and gave me the simplest of tasks to just take the pass and go over by the posts; it was so easy, I was handed the ball and was straight through. Scrums were something else in those days and gaining possession from ones that were contested was a vital part of the game. That afternoon, Barry was sensational in his primary task, completely overshadowing his opposite number. Everybody packed down and shoved and the hooker had to time his strike to perfection and Barry won the ball so many times against the head that it was embarrassing. With all the quality possession he secured for us, it was not surprising that we dominated.

It's hard to pick out specific matches from so long ago, but during the 'big freeze' of 1963 we managed to get a game on at Castleford in the first round of the Challenge Cup. They had braziers all over the field to ensure it went ahead, but it was still like playing on concrete. There must have been a hundred and sixty of them on there, trying to defrost the pitch - drills were even used at one stage to try and break up the surface. Then, just before kick-off, the braziers were all removed, which left ashes and all sorts on the field. The couple of yards around where each of the fires had been was soft for a little while - it was a bit like playing on a chess board - but they froze back up almost straight away. Cas so wanted the game to take place, with it being Leeds at home on the road to Wembley. They were rewarded with a packed ground and the players just had to put up with it. Unfortunately for them, their efforts came to nought and we scrapped through. I even managed to skate over for one of our tries.

By the end of the 1964 season, after twelve hugely enjoyable years at Leeds, I took up an option to go over to

Australia to player-coach in the Metropolitan League, with Wentworthville.

They had decided to develop the club a couple of years before they got me over and applied for a license to play in the senior competition. But they had always been a junior set-up and didn't even have a proper clubhouse at that time. When I got there they had built a single storey, comfortable facility, catering for sport-minded members. It overlooked the rugby ground but there was also a bowling club, table tennis, snooker and basketball. Eventually they applied to the New South Wales Rugby League for promotion into the second tier of competition. The governing body's intention was eventually to have two clubs from there go into the ARL first-grade premiership.

In the time I was there, it just so happened that we had the best players. I was very fortunate and we won the division in seven out of my eight seasons. Penrith and Cronulla were among the easy beats, but they were the ones who subsequently got the nod into the big time. Initially, we were told it would be us, but geography won the day. Cronulla were south of Sydney and Penrith off to the west, whereas we were no more than a mile from Parramatta. Wentworthville's exclusion was probably the only really sad thing that happened to me in my rugby life. Derek Hallas was at Parramatta for some of the time I was out there, before he came back home, but I rarely bumped into him and his wife, Barbara.

On one occasion, in 1968, I played in a curtain-raiser to a Great Britain World Cup match down under. The oddest thing was playing in front of 70,000 people at the Sydney Cricket Ground in a domestic game; Wentworthville didn't normally attract that many. At half-time, I recall a couple of the British lads - Mick Shoebottom and his partner-in-crime and room-mate 'Flash' Flanagan - popping over for a chat.

King of Rugger

My kids, Kevin and Karen, were dismayed when we decided to come home, because they'd had all of their formative years over in Australia. It was difficult for them having been brought up there for eight glorious years but they both realised then, and do now, that it was for the best of intentions, to secure their further education. They both got good degrees that they wouldn't have got in Australia, because the best standard of education at that level was undoubtedly in the universities back here. Kevin and Karen had the choice of a few and have done well in the ensuing years. Those times in Australia, though, were arguably the best of my life. The lifestyle and teaching out there suited me and I am often invited back to reunions to celebrate those good old days, because if you do right by them, they do the same by you. While I was there, I taught in a mixed High School. There were no disciplinary problems and teaching itself was a joy. Apart from maths, I was given the job of preparing teams for inter-school rugby league competitions.

On returning to Leeds in 1972, I applied to the local education authority for employment and, although I told them that I was prepared to give time to coach rugby on evenings and Saturdays, those extra-curricular activities were of little value when they sent me to an all-girls High School at Silver Royds. Remarkably, though, I survived fifteen years there until my retirement and it was another very happy period of life. It was not a very macho environment but bearable! Rugby-wise, although I enjoyed being in the company of the fraternity, I soon found that I didn't have the enthusiasm necessary to coach. After a season with the 'A' team at Leeds and a spell with the first team at Dewsbury, the commitment was missing and it came to a sad end on both occasions.

Looking back on an eventful time in the sport, it was luck rather than good judgement that got me to where I was and

I wouldn't swap the life I've had with anybody. I didn't bother to think about accolades, except that there is now a suite in the new Carnegie Stand at Headingley and a pub in the ground at Gorseinon, where I first started playing, named after me. That, together with honorary membership of the Taverners at Leeds, is more than enough.

It is very difficult to determine just how good players are today compared to my time, because of the superb physical condition that they are in thanks to full-time training. We wouldn't have lasted more than five minutes in Super League. But, having said that, I would have loved to have seen my contemporaries honed to that standard of fitness.

There have also been so many rule changes that equating the different eras is impossible. For example, there is the loss of contested scrums; the introduction of substitutes (which has turned rugby league into a seventeen-a-side rather than thirteen-a-side game); the use of kicking tees and differently weighted and flighted balls. Whether it is all for the good, I don't know. I'm sure I would have loved the 40-20 kick, but I'm still not convinced that summer is when we should be playing rugby. I'm not a fan of flat passes and am still to be convinced about the value of the video referee, but Friday night's at Headingley Carnegie are still something special. When I played, the likes of Featherstone Rovers, Hunslet and Oldham were the lifeblood. Today, those famous names seem to have gone by the board.

I used to enjoy a cigarette, which you can't imagine now. It was part of my pre-match and occasionally even half-time routine. I was brought up in a religious household with my father being a lay preacher and my upbringing was strict, so when I went to do national service I was introduced to a more relaxed environment and I took advantage of the cheap naval Woodbines available on board ship. I suppose you could say that I smoked heavily – Players Number One and Capstan Full Strength - but it was never a consideration that it might have an effect. Cliff Morgan, when he was on the speaking circuit, used to mention it. Whenever I meet up with him he invariably reminds me: 'I remember you, Jonesy, walking out to play an international and going down the steps to the pitch, and you putting your fag out on the wall'. But that was the way it was back then. It didn't seem to make any difference to the standard of rugby we played.

I don't think about my points scoring records at all and whether or not they will be surpassed. It doesn't mean anything, simply because of the reasons why you can't make direct comparisons - even the points values are different for a try and a drop-goal. If someone like Kevin Sinfield overtakes me at Leeds, fantastic and good luck to him. When I started playing union, a drop-goal was worth four points, the most you could score, but emphases change.

When I signed for Leeds, I had no conception that I would be there for twelve years - my only thought was how was I going to spend the sign-on money and I achieved that in a year! I enjoyed doing that, but it might have been why I had to stay for the next eleven afterwards.

I've been so lucky in my life, not least in my marriage. My kids are the best you could ever wish for and I've got three brilliant grandchildren carrying the flag for the next generation. I've been incredibly fortunate. The only bad luck I've had was when Maureen passed away in 1987. I never went home to Wales, although I did miss a lot of things that I used to have and do, not least the Gower Peninsula. I'd often ride down there on my bike and go for a swim, it is one of the nicest parts of the world. It wasn't commercialised in those days and the only way you could get down to it was to cycle. It is a magnificent coastline, just to the west of Swansea.

Coming back from Australia, we had the choice to locate

anywhere, but there was only one option really and that was to return to Leeds where we had made our home. I knew people up here and my kids were born and bred Yorkshire folk. They returned to familiar schooling and we just settled back in.

The arrival of Celtic Crusaders in Super League could herald a breakthrough in Wales for rugby league. We have always been told that there is so much talent to be brought to the fore but teams don't rely solely on local players. Leeds have always been cosmopolitan in their make-up. When I arrived to don the famous blue and amber colours we had Aussies, Kiwis and a Scot about the place, and only really 'Shanks' Watson could be termed local, until Jeff Stevenson arrived. Imports, like me, have always been part of the game.

I can't have any regrets about switching codes all those years ago. I wasn't thinking so much about the challenge, more that there was something else to do. It must have been for the money in those days because I had no future at home in Wales. I was driving a dumper or a lorry on-site at the Carmarthen Bay power station that they were building. I had to cash in on the one thing I was best at doing - being able to kick a bloody ball! I was also credited with developing a 'hanging pass' but I don't know what is meant by that. The ball might have appeared to be suspended in mid-air, but it was just a runaround with the scrum-half.

To be honest, I never thought about anything I did on the field. I just went out and played for the enjoyment of playing. To some, I might have appeared to be nonchalant. But Maureen, if she was here, would tell you that I must have been hell to live with on a Saturday morning.

As told to PHIL CAPLAN